"With her usual warmth and compassion, Mary Hunt takes the fear out of an often-terrifying topic. Any woman who's ever wanted to be able to retire confidently can benefit from the down-to-earth knowledge in this book."

—**Liz Pulliam Weston**, *MSN Money* columnist and author of *The 10 Commandments of Money*

"From cover to cover, an informative and even delightful read on a tough-to-face subject! In her personal style, Mary cuts to the chase on exactly how to make the most of the opportunities and resources you have today, so that you can sail through the golden years. Mary holds your hand and walks you through it step by step. Just what I needed right now! Thank you, Mary!"

—**Teri Gault**, CEO and founder, TheGroceryGame.com

"*The Smart Woman's Guide to Planning for Retirement* takes the fear out of financial planning and gives women a financial blueprint they can relate to. Any women who read this book will walk away confident and in control of their finances."

—**Ellen Breslau**, editor-in-chief, Grandparents.com

"You don't have to live in fear of your future in retirement. *The Smart Woman's Guide to Planning for Retirement* brings clarity to all your financial questions. Mary Hunt feels like a friend sharing hope for the future."

—**Melissa Montana**, CEO/president, STAR Educational Media Network

"Powerful, practical, and solid advice on facing retirement with confidence. Apply Mary Hunt's knowledge and you'll feel empowered."

—**Gerri Detweiler**, nationally recognized credit expert and host of *Talk Credit Radio*

THE SMART WOMAN'S GUIDE TO PLANNING FOR RETIREMENT

Other Books by Mary Hunt

7 Money Rules for Life
Raising Financially Confident Kids
Debt-Proof Your Christmas
Cheaper, Better, Faster

THE SMART WOMAN'S GUIDE

to PLANNING *for* RETIREMENT

HOW *to* SAVE *for* YOUR FUTURE TODAY

Mary Hunt

Revell

a division of Baker Publishing Group
Grand Rapids, Michigan

Published by Revell
a division of Baker Publishing Group
P.O. Box 6287, Grand Rapids, MI 49516-6287
www.revellbooks.com

Printed in the United States of America

Library of Congress Cataloging-in-Publication Data is on file at the Library of Congress, Washington, DC.

ISBN 978-0-8007-2113-8 (cloth)

Scripture quotations are from the Holy Bible, New International Version®. NIV®. Copyright © 1973, 1978, 1984, 2011 by Biblica, Inc.™ Used by permission of Zondervan. All rights reserved worldwide. www.zondervan.com

To protect the privacy of those who have shared their stories with the author, some details and names have been changed.

13 14 15 16 17 18 19   7 6 5 4 3 2 1

*For Lauren and millions of women
who need to save for retirement.*

Contents

Contents

Preface

Throughout this book, I refer to you, my dear reader, as "you" and to myself as "me." If you are married, please consider this a plural "you" that includes your husband, your financial partner. This aspect of your relationship is so important because married people who behave as true financial partners do better financially.[1] A healthy marriage promotes financial success both now and in the future.

In the same way, when I refer to "myself," "my mortgage," "my savings and investments," I really mean "ours." Harold and I have been married for forty-three years. To have constantly written "you and your husband if you are married, or just you if you are single, or you and your ex if you are divorced, or you and the estate of your first husband" together with "my husband, Harold, and I" would have become annoyingly awkward. I'm annoyed just describing it. So when you come to these references, please adapt them to be compatible with your marital status.

For my non–US readers, while you may not have Social Security or other specific US programs, every major Western economy has the same types of issues and programs that future retirees must consider. The information in this book transcends our borders, which will make it useful for all.

Acknowledgments

Over the past two decades, I have written a number of books but none as challenging as this one. I gave up regularly and even threw in the towel once, certain I could not do it. But the subject matter became very personal, and the more I waded into these murky waters, the more life-impacting the book became.

I am grateful beyond words to my editor and friend, Vicki Crumpton, who would not let me give up and extended uncommon patience to prove it.

Thank you to Cathy Hollenbeck, who got me back in the saddle more than once with instructions to "Just ride!" Thanks for the tough love.

Many thanks to all of my dear friends who held me up in prayer during the months they didn't hear much from me. You know who you are.

To my husband, Harold, the most long-suffering man on earth—I'm excited about the next season of our lives. Thanks for your undying support and love. I cannot imagine doing life without you, nor can I imagine our future without all I learned and experienced in the process of writing this book. I love you more now than ever before.

Introduction

Something's wrong. According to a 2012 survey, 92 percent of women of all ages in the United States don't feel they know enough to reach their retirement savings goals. This lack of education can't be because there aren't enough books on the subject. Search "retirement" on the popular online bookseller Amazon and you'll find more than twenty thousand results.

And there is no shortage of workshops, speakers, advisors, brokers, counselors, and financial planners offering retirement planning services. Retirement planning has become a billion-dollar industry in the United States. An online search for "retirement calculators" provides thousands of options as well.

So why isn't any of this working? Why is it that only 8 percent of women believe they know what to do?

With all these available resources, you may be wondering why on earth I'd consider adding another retirement book to the already crowded field. Because I think women need a different kind of book, one without all the jargon, charts, and mind-numbing data, one that simply and honestly cuts through the complicated information that's out there and provides just the facts and motivation they need in a warm and conversational way—the way we'd chat over coffee about something that is very important to both of us.

Big Surprise Ahead

Millions of women approaching retirement age have nothing stored up for when they won't be able to work for a living. They think Social Security will be enough, but they are in for a rude awakening.

A more common attitude is, "I've got plenty of time. I'll catch up when I get the bills paid. We've got a wedding coming up and a child in college, and we have to help our parents." Retirement is far away and other things are so much more pressing that it's easy to sacrifice the important for the urgent.

Some married women blithely assume their husbands have this retirement thing all covered and that they'll be cared for. Others just treat it like a big joke, saying they're planning to win the lottery or get a big inheritance. And on it goes for years, then more years, and before they know it, the sixties are knocking on the door. They're worried and terrified of what will happen to them because they have less than five hundred dollars in the bank and a pathetically small balance in the retirement account.

I don't know what your excuses might be, but you're not the only one who has them. I've had them myself.

Right now, I feel like a highway flagman. You're over there in the fast lane, distracted by all the noise of life, and I'm over here with this big red flag, doing everything I can to get your attention. There's big trouble up ahead.

Women, in general, are not prepared, and it's not pretty. Fifty-five percent of women depend on Social Security alone, with no retirement savings at all.[1] The average monthly Social

Security check is $1,130. Let me put that into perspective. If you work forty hours a week for $1,130 per month, you're making $6.40 per hour. The federal minimum wage is $7.25 per hour. Could you live on that?

Other women retire with some savings, and the average amount is less than $30,000. If you live to age eighty-five, that amounts to an additional $125 a month.[2] Is that really any better?

You need to get out of the fast lane. You won't have smooth sailing unless you make a course correction. I want to guide you to another, safer route so that when you arrive at the "retirement" off-ramp you'll be prepared and ready for the best season of life.

Ladies, we must do what we do best: take charge. The question is how. How do you balance one more thing when you are already so heavily burdened? How do you plan for thirty years down the road when you'd be happy just to get through the chaos of the day—getting everyone to school, then you to work, then everyone back home in time for dinner, so you can get everyone to bed, just to start all over again tomorrow?

If you're overspending, or in debt, or feel your finances are out of control, trust me, I understand. While I can't *make* you change the way you're living and spending now, I can show you *how* to do just that. As you read this book, I hope you develop an urgency in your heart that will stop you in your tracks and keep you from spending all that you have now to create space for future planning.

If you feel fearful, undisciplined, or uneducated when it comes to managing your money, you can change all that. The first step is to read this book with a strong resolve to do what it says no matter how difficult it may seem. Doing so might just save you from years of misery and poverty.

Failure, the Best Teacher?

Money mistakes. We all make them, but some of us make really big ones that take us years to recover from, if ever. Some mistakes can never be fixed. I know. I've made some doozies in my life.

I'm not here to complain about the mistakes I've made. That would be another mistake. Mistakes are useful because they teach us what doesn't work. But making the same mistake over and over again while expecting different results—well, that's the definition of insanity. The secret is to learn from our mistakes and then move on, knowing not to do the same things again.

My money mistakes have been costly not just financially but in terms of time, stress, and emotional turmoil. I have scars. I could make a list of the things I won't do again because I've proven they do not work.

I'd like to say I learned my lesson from each one the first time, no repeats. I can't. I'm often a slow learner. And stubborn. But I am grateful for all that I learned, for the ways God redeemed even the mistakes to bring me to the place I am right now in my life, right here with you, taking the mistakes of the past and turning them into something good and positive for the future.

While mistakes can be great teachers, there may be an even better way to learn. A recent university study[3] examined the experiences of cardiovascular surgeons to determine whether success or failure was the better teacher and whose failure provided better lessons. The study produced a striking conclusion. Failure is the best teacher mostly when someone else has failed. Surgeons learned best from their own successes and the failures of others; their own failures were much harder to learn from.

You do not have the time or the money to learn from making your own mistakes. That's why I am offering to let you learn from my failures. I've done all the hard work of making lots of mistakes. Let me save you time and money. Benefit from my mistakes, and you'll be miles ahead. And if you've already committed your share of blunders, let's call this a new day—a place to pick yourself up and to start again.

1

My Wake-up Call

Never ask, Can I do this? Instead ask, How can I do this?

LaRae Quy

I was mostly daydreaming when it hit. It was an emotional jolt with the sensation I would expect from being struck by lightning. I'd been gathering data and statistics in preparation to write this book, but at that moment my heart was not in it.

I considered approaching the subject with humor. I was thinking of pithy zingers like, "I will never be over the hill. I'm too tired to climb it!" Or, "Middle age: that time when you finally get your head together and your body starts falling apart!" And I'd lobby hard for this title: *Real Women Don't Have Hot Flashes; They Have Power Surges!*

That still makes me laugh.

As I was thinking about all of this while rummaging through websites and publications relating to retirement, the official sign-up window for Medicare applicants caught my attention. On a lark, I decided to figure out the month and year that I, your humble, much younger author, would be ready to hang it up and prepare for the end.

There I was, sitting at my desk, half staring out the window, thinking to myself that every car in the parking lot was black, and working on a mental grocery list. That's when I got a rush of adrenaline that made my heart pound.

Calm down, I told myself. I must have put in the wrong birth year. Yeah, that had to be it.

I started over and came up with the same result. I couldn't believe it. Nine months from that exact day my window of opportunity to sign up for Medicare would open. Nine months! That's 270 days. It might as well have been the next day for how close it felt.

Let me explain something. It's not like I don't know my age. And yes, I am aware that Medicare is for people who have reached the age of threescore and five. But this was the first time in my life that those two facts converged on the highway of life, with my name splattered all over the collision.

For the longest time I just sat there, stunned. Why didn't I see this coming? It's not like I hadn't thought about retirement or even made a few plans here and there. But it was always so far away—like in another lifetime. I would deal with it later at a more convenient time. Why waste my youth worrying or planning for something over which I had no control?

When finally I could speak, I informed my husband.

"I've entered the sunset of my life," I said.

"What brought that on?"

"Nine months . . . I have only nine months before my final act."

And in my mind, I became a fully developed senior citizen.

My wake-up call was not the kind of gentle tap on the shoulder your mom might give you to let you know that dinner is ready. I'm talking about a kind of wake-up call that blasts you out of a sound sleep, sets your heart racing, and puts your mind into overdrive. My emotions were all over the place. Fear, panic, dread—you name it. If it was an unpleasant feeling, I had it in spades.

How did this happen? How could my life just sneak up on me like that? My reaction was overly dramatic, I can see that now. But it was real and something I will never forget. I am grateful, too, because it jerked me out of my fantasies. Am I the only woman on earth who secretly assumed she would never have to deal with the issues of retirement? While I don't think I ever uttered the words, in my heart I knew I was too young to be old. And I would do anything to remain "not old" forever.

Over the years, I'd had much calmer and gentler wake-up calls, which I chose to ignore. It took this call with all the force of a ship's horn to get my attention.

Have you had a retirement wake-up call? I can promise you they intensify with age. Had I paid attention in my twenties, I would have responded to that sweet, tender voice that suggested I put ten dollars a week into an aggressive investment program. Another call came in my thirties when a very kind employer set up a plan for me to invest in real estate. Did I respond? No. I believed I couldn't afford to participate. I would do that when I got my finances straightened out. I could go on and on, but I think you get my point.

Wake-up calls can take many forms. It might be the annual statement from your tax-advantaged retirement account that projects what you'll have in there by the time you retire, or it might be your estimated benefits statement from the Social

Security office. It doesn't have to take something severe to get you thinking about and planning for the future. In fact, smart women don't procrastinate. They take action, even if only by taking baby steps. This book could be the gentle call you need to wake up and get going.

I've learned a lot over the years but nothing more important than this: Failure to plan is expensive. Choosing to anticipate is the way to head off the big financial blows, because you are buying a commodity more precious than money: time.

I don't think it is a mere coincidence that I am writing this and you are reading it. Our paths have crossed for a purpose. I cannot know for certain what challenges you are facing or where you are in your life story, but the subject of saving for retirement has brought us together.

As for my age, I'm back to not caring about it that much. Moving into this next season of my life has been remarkably painless because I know that I get to bring the wisdom and experiences of my life with me into this new adventure. And that has filled me with a sense of excitement and purpose.

2

You've Already Got
What It Takes

I can do all this through him who gives me strength.

Philippians 4:13

I learned to drive a car before driver's ed classes and driving schools. I had a handbook from the Department of Motor Vehicles, a patient father, and a burning desire to get my license.

I studied that handbook until both of us were ragged. I knew the rules and laws inside out and upside down. Even so, I was a nervous wreck on the day of my driving examination.

What if they ask questions I don't know?

What if I forget everything I do know?

What if my mind goes blank and I forget how to read?

My desire to get my license was stronger than my fear of failure, though. That's what got me through the door and into the line at the DMV to take the written test. If I passed it, I would take a behind-the-wheel examination with a police officer in the passenger seat.

I opened the test booklet and glanced at the first multiple choice question. Without even looking at the choices, I knew the answer. Same for the next question, and the next. Suddenly, this feeling of confidence came over me. It wasn't arrogant or egotistical. And I wasn't overconfident. I just knew that I knew the answers. My confidence was a quiet, knowing sense of certainty. Knowledge gave me the power I needed to trust myself to make the right choices. I had *certitude* (oh, how I love that word—a cross between certainty and attitude).

I aced the written test and then convincingly demonstrated to the examining officer that I could safely drive and parallel park a motor vehicle. I did it. I got my license on the first try.

That day my confidence soared, not in a cocky or arrogant way but in a way that I knew I could be trusted to react appropriately and make the right decisions while driving a car. I knew with certainty.

How does this all relate to women and retirement planning?

It has been well documented that retirement confidence among women lags behind that of men.[1] A survey conducted in 2012 revealed that 92 percent of women of all ages do not feel educated enough to reach their retirement savings goals.[2]

I will never believe that when it comes to the subject of retirement we females suddenly turn stupid. That we can't understand concepts such as "return on money," "draw-down rates," and "delayed gratification." We are not competent in managing an investment portfolio. We are not capable of consistently saving money in anticipation of our years in retirement. We cannot speak intelligently with a financial planner. We are not capable of determining the best time to begin drawing Social Security benefits. We cannot research and make intelligent decisions regarding which Medicare plan will be the most beneficial.

Of course we can do these things. If we lack confidence, it's because we lack knowledge and desire, certainly not because we lack intelligence and ability.

Look, you are a smart woman. If you need proof, it says so right on the cover of this book. You will not be a victim of statistics. Statistical data is used to create big-picture views, but the results of surveys and studies are not reliable for individual situations.

You don't really believe that out of ten of your friends only .8 of one of you is financially confident, do you? It's like the infamous family with 2.5 children. I've never met a .5 child or a .8 woman. Do you see what I'm saying?

You don't have to sit back hoping and praying that you're not part of the 92 percent. And you are not doomed because some statistic says the poverty rate of women sixty-five and older is nearly two times higher than that of men. You have free will and a strong mind. Retirement planning takes determination and hard work, but I promise that you have what it takes to become insanely confident.

I don't need fancy studies to convince me that men and women are not wired the same way. But I do enjoy learning why male and female brains process things so differently.

As a woman, embedded within you is a fundamental need that goes to the heart and soul of this matter of retirement planning. According to psychologist and author Willard F. Harley, all humans are born with basic needs. Women need financial security—enough money to live comfortably. It's a basic need in women, while most men do not have this need.[3]

If you've ever wondered why your husband doesn't share your sense of urgency about retirement planning, this may be the reason. He's just not wired to put retirement planning as high on his list of priorities as you are. What this means is that you may be the one who is best suited to take on the task of spearheading financial planning for the partnership by learning all you can to create and implement a plan.

If, on the other hand, you are single, this should come as good news if you've assumed all along that without a husband you're doomed for lack of financial support. Sure, you have the inborn need for financial security, but (as you're about to learn) you also have the ability to meet that need.

Just think about this. As a woman:

- You've been uniquely designed by your Creator to care for small things, nurturing, loving, and encouraging them to grow up to be healthy and wise. It's in your nature.

- You are predisposed to organize, plan, and execute complex tasks. If you've ever given birth, you may have experienced this about forty-eight hours before the big event when something went off in your mind that insisted you needed to clean out the pantry, reorganize the garage, and give the kitchen a quick coat of paint. It's instinct, a surge of energy often referred to as "nesting."

- You are strong, determined, clever, and above all resilient. You have amazing inborn talents and abilities. You're like a Maserati driven only on a city street. You have horsepower you've never tapped.

- Your temperament—the way you think, behave, and react to life—is much different from that of men. Our brains process things in opposing ways.[4]

Girl, you have what it takes to become confident. It's in your DNA, a blessing of your gender. It's been said that women have the responsibility gene! I am not making this stuff up. The differences between men and women have been studied and documented, the results of which I continue to find amazing but not altogether surprising.

When it comes to the specifics of money management and retirement planning:

- Women are better equipped mentally and emotionally than men to manage and invest money.
- Women have the temperament to set financial goals and also to achieve them.
- Women, instinctively, are more observant and detail oriented.
- Women have a greater capacity for self-control and personal discipline.
- Women are less likely to panic and act irrationally when a situation comes up that requires a nonemotionally based decision.
- Women age particularly well, becoming mellower, calmer, and more accepting and satisfied with age.
- Women are more averse to risk. Compared to men, women have a lower tolerance for risk. This makes women well suited for managing investments, because unlike men, who often have an appetite for risk and trading too much, women are willing to wait things out.
- Women are nurturers. It comes naturally for women to feel responsible for husbands, kids, friends, aging parents, and pets. This translates easily into the same kind of caring needed for investments and retirement accounts.
- Women ask for directions. Research shows that women are aware of their lack of financial knowledge and are more willing to ask for advice than men. Men see asking for help as a sign of weakness, but women see it as

a rational thing to do because it can lead to making smarter decisions.[5]

- Women take fewer financial risks than men do but not because they're wusses. Both sexes secrete the hormone oxytocin in stressful situations, but women secrete more of it, which helps them stay calmer.

- Women write stuff down. They keep diaries, write in their journals, and keep track of important details on their calendars.

- Women display better judgment than their counterpart males, particularly when it comes to money. A twenty-something young woman is more likely to sign up for a 401(k) retirement plan than her twentysomething male co-worker who's more interested in the latest electronic gadgetry than long-term investing.[6]

- Women are persistent. When women set challenging goals, which they are more likely to do than men, they stick to them and see them through to a successful conclusion.

I didn't learn to drive a car by dreaming about it. Writing "I really want to get my driver's license" on a sheet of paper didn't get the job done. Actually, I did both of those things, but stopping there would have made my goal nothing more than a dream.

I became a confident driver because I memorized the handbook and practiced driving and parking a car. My confidence prepared me to make quick decisions and to react appropriately under all kinds of driving conditions. Had I only dreamed about driving a car but done nothing to learn how to do it, you can be sure I never would have attained the confidence necessary to become a good driver.

Confidence is fueled by the power that comes with knowledge. That's the confidence women need when it comes to personal finances and money management. That's the confidence we need as we approach the subject of retirement.

Dreaming about traveling and spending time with family during your retirement years is not going to give you the confidence you need to achieve it. You have to do something about it, starting now.

It's time to stop procrastinating. Any reason you might have to put off learning about and saving for retirement is just an excuse. It is not valid. You need to learn everything you can now about personal finance and money management. That knowledge will help you develop confidence—that quiet knowing that you can trust yourself to make wise decisions and good judgment calls—no matter what your situation might be. This is how smart women think.

3

A Lifetime Money Plan

A [wo]man who wants to do something will find a way; a
[wo]man who doesn't will find an excuse.

Stephen Dolley Jr.

If you want to enjoy the perfect retirement, you must live
the perfect life. That means you never lose your job, and
recessions never happen. Stock market crashes happen only
after you've cashed out, and housing prices soar just before
you sell, then plunge to historic lows on the day you find
your dream retirement home. You never know an unexpected
expense because you have the uncanny ability to expect the
unexpected. You never divorce, never experience a financial
disaster, and always spend less than you earn.

In this perfect retirement world, you max out your contributions to your retirement accounts starting in your twenties,
you never get sick or miss a day of work, and your kids receive
full college scholarships. You have accounts set up for every

child's wedding, pay cash for all your cars, and know with uncommon precision exactly what things will cost in the future. And you save for them accordingly. There it is—the perfect life.

In the real world, there is no such thing as perfection. What you can do, however, is start paying attention to your financial health in the same way you should be taking good care of your physical health.

Retirement isn't a separate part of life. It's a phase of life, and while you may or may not continue working full-time, you will go on living. How you care for your financial health starting now is going to make a big difference then.

Let me tell you about a couple of women I know.

My friend Traci had a heart attack at forty-two. That she survived was nothing short of a miracle, according to her doctor. The heart attack was massive, and she blamed it on her genetic heritage, something over which she had no control.

The attack got her attention, but her real wake-up call came months later at a follow-up visit when the doctor sternly suggested that her lifestyle was the biggest contributing factor, not her genes. Her family history pointed to the fact that she was predisposed to heart disease, but her doctor refused to let her off the hook. She lived on junk food, smoked two packs a day, and as an insurance broker, did a lot of sitting behind a desk. She decided to get serious about her health, but her idea of "serious" was to walk around the block a couple of times a week. Sadly, she didn't change her lifestyle habits. At age forty-five, she had coronary bypass surgery followed closely by a debilitating stroke.

Eleanor, mother of another friend, always took really good care of her health. She was careful about what and how much she ate, never smoked, and walked three miles a day, rain or shine. Eleanor was diagnosed with breast cancer in her early forties and survived a double mastectomy, several rounds of chemotherapy, radiation, restorative surgeries, and a thirty-five-year regimen of the cancer inhibitor Tamoxifen. At age ninety-two, her daily walks have become shorter, but she remains remarkably healthy and very active in her retirement community, where she lives independently and enjoys a rich and rewarding life.

Neither Traci nor Eleanor could do a thing about their genetic predispositions to life-threatening diseases. But both had full control over the lifestyle choices they made every day. Traci abused her health, while Eleanor took good care of hers. Traci paid dearly for her choices in pain, suffering, and diminished options, while Eleanor was rewarded with a full and active life for hers. Traci became functionally disabled at fifty-four; Eleanor is still living strong.

Financial Health

Physical health is similar to financial health. No matter the hand you're dealt, if you make good choices by living below your means, saving consistently, and shunning debt starting at a young age, they will pay off with good financial health in your retirement years.

Not surprisingly, when you think about it, good health is one of the best ways to keep your expenses low as you enter the retirement years. And we are learning that good financial health is really good for your physical health as well.

A medical study reported by Reuters Health discovered that owing money to credit card companies is not only bad for your bank balance but also may be bad for your health. This study concluded that credit card debt—especially if that debt is a high proportion of your yearly income—increases the likelihood of having health problems.[1]

Years of overspending, not saving, and carrying loads of consumer debt are to your financial health what years of smoking, junk food, and little exercise are to your physical health. And the onset of poor health can lead to financial hardship, which in turn can lead to an increase in stress, which will itself perpetuate more health problems. See? Health and finances are inextricably connected.

The best way to prepare for retirement is to take care of yourself and your money each and every day. The surest way to do that is to live according to a sensible lifetime money plan starting when you are young.

But what if you've wasted a lot of years not taking care of your financial health? What if, just as Traci's unhealthy lifestyle wreaked havoc on her health, your financial lifestyle has done a number on your financial health? I'll tell you what Traci's doctor told her: start now. Stop making bad choices and start making good ones. Just do it.

A physical examination by a qualified health professional measures and assesses a person's physical health. I've had a few physicals in my life, so I know the routine. I'll bet you do too.

First, it's the blood pressure, then "Please step on the scale," followed by specimens to calculate cholesterol levels. An EKG is not unusual, and there's the treadmill, mammography machine, and dreaded camera-on-a-pole procedure (thankfully, we get to sleep through that one).

I have never had a doctor call me into her office and suggest that I just pour all of my resources and energy into raising my family and getting everyone educated, married off, and set up in their own homes before I think about my own health and well-being. I've never heard the words, "Don't worry about your weight or your high blood pressure now. And that plaque in your arteries? Everyone these days seems to have plenty of it—it's difficult to avoid. You'll have plenty of time to figure things out later. It will work out somehow."

Doctors aren't like that. My primary care physician is intolerant of high blood pressure, insisting that mine should be as low as it was the day I turned twenty-one. He has a kind way of encouraging me to keep taking off the pounds. And he will cleverly slip into the conversation, "What kind of exercise are we doing these days?" He's the kind of doctor who calls me a few days later with the results of my blood work. He would never think of waiting a few years to get around to that, especially if he were to see something unusual or alarming.

I don't enjoy mammograms and colonoscopies. But believing as I do that early detection is the secret to continued good health, I have them. I make sure to show up at my appointments because I care deeply about my physical health. I make it a habit to take care of my health now, hoping that my good health will help take care of me and my finances later.

We know that physical and financial health are both important to our overall well-being and in many ways intertwined. But I don't know of many women who get a financial checkup every year or so the way they get mammograms and routine physicals.

I am happy to let you know that a routine financial assessment for the purpose of retirement saving is not nearly as invasive or time consuming as a medical checkup. And you don't have to slip into a lovely paper gown or perch yourself on anything that includes stirrups.

A financial health examination looks at how you're managing your money, the level of your emergency fund, your debt, and your retirement accounts and investments. In fact, if you'd like to step into my office, we can go straight to the steps you need to begin taking now to ace your retirement savings plan.

A Retirement Savings Plan

There are six specific strategies you need to follow to build your financial health now and to see you through all of your tomorrows—before and after you retire, no matter your age or marital status. These six strategies are the heart and soul of this book. This is your retirement savings plan. You cannot get started too soon, but you can wait too long.

1. Develop a money management system.
2. Build an emergency fund.
3. Get out of debt.
4. Maximize your retirement accounts.
5. Own your home outright.
6. Build your personal investment portfolio.

In the chapters that follow, we are going to dig into all six of these strategies. We are going to learn how to follow them and how to keep on track through all the seasons and ups and downs of life.

Developing these six areas in your life will make you strong, fit, and lean so that you will be able to move seamlessly into whatever kind of retirement you choose when the time comes. Improving your financial health now is going to pay off big in terms of more options later, plus peace of mind.

If you are in your twenties or thirties, getting financially healthy is going to be much easier than for those in the forties and fifties who may be just now considering their financial health. Because you are starting young, you will not have to shed years of bad habits and lost opportunities. You will not have to take off the kind of financial weight that comes with the consequences of having made really bad decisions. Because you're starting young, you will not have to make the kinds of sacrifices others will. So I applaud you and want you to know how proud I am of you for seeing the need to begin saving now for retirement. You are demonstrating wisdom beyond your age.

For you, dear readers, who are not so young, who have not taken care of your financial health and are now reaping the consequences of bad decisions and lost opportunites, I know about this kind of thing. I took twelve of the most potentially productive years of my life and blew them to smithereens by racking up more than $100,000 in debt. Then it took me thirteen years to repair the damage. Add it up. That's twenty-five years to get back to zero. I know something about being financially out of shape. And I know a lot about making up for lost time and changing the course of my life. It can be done. It is not going to be as easy as it will be for those who are at the start of their careers and life choices. It may require sacrifice on your part and a lot of sweat and tears. But you can do it.

I carry the scars of a dark and painful financial past. I've had my battles with the fallout of making poor health choices as well. As you know, it took me thirteen years to repay more than $100,000 of consumer debt. As a result, I began to see the parallels between bad physical health and bad financial health and began addressing my problem of obesity. Sure, the tendency runs through my genes, but I was totally responsible for my lifestyle choices.

Since 1999, I have shed ninety pounds. I have ten to go. I am on track to make it to one hundred pounds in thirteen years, which has an uncanny similarity to having paid back $100,000 in thirteen years. I've repaid debt, and I've lost weight. For me, paying back the debt and getting financially healthy was much easier than losing weight and reclaiming my physical health.

Every woman who has ever stopped smoking, lost a pound, began exercising, or turned the tables on her poor financial health started by giving up that first cigarette, losing that first pound, walking that first mile, and saving that first dollar.

Change only comes when you take that first step. Then you take another. And another and another until you achieve a life change. Crash diets and crash financial fixes don't work. Going on the Popcorn Grapefruit Diet is sure to cause a big weight loss, but that's not a sustainable eating plan because it is not realistic.

Developing these six areas in your financial life will not provide quick fixes. This is not a crash fiscal diet. What I propose to you in the coming chapters is a new way of life that will help you build the strong financial base you will need to carry yourself through retirement, regardless of when and how you decide that will happen.

You might be thinking that this sounds hard. I'll be honest. Depending on your age and the extent to which you have been ignoring your financial health, it may be challenging. And the older you are, the more difficult it may be. You will not have the luxury of time to ease into change.

But what are your alternatives?

You can slip into denial and go on pretending that somehow things will just work out. Or you can choose to get into the best financial shape possible so you can look forward to enjoying financial stability in your future.

Make a commitment to start now, right where you are and while you are able. Work at building this financial base now—like you've never worked before—so you won't have to work when you're eighty if you don't want to.

When I was a kid, jumping rope was my favorite school recess activity. You could jump single or double, and we had all kinds of rhymes and rules. But the ultimate challenge was the scariest game of all: Double Dutch, a game in which one or more players jump two long ropes turning in opposite directions. And the faster the better.

It was one thing for the jumpers and rope turners to all start at the same time, but it was quite another for the turners to get going at the fastest speed possible and then the jumpers running into those blazing fast ropes, jumping as fast as they could and all the while not missing a beat. When everything went exactly right, it was so much fun.

When I talk to women about retirement saving, most tell me they wish they had started planning and saving sooner. If you're twenty, you have the luxury of starting from a standing position, slow and easy. Over time, your speed and technique will naturally improve. If you're in your forties or fifties and just now getting into the game, you can't wait any longer. The whipping ropes of life are not going to slow down. You have to go in. Just take a deep breath, get a running start, and jump as fast as you can.

4

Develop a
Money Management System

The amount of money you have has got nothing to do with what you earn. People earning a million dollars a year can have no money. People earning $35,000 a year can be quite well off. It's not what you earn, it's what you spend.

Paul Clitheroe

The first step to getting financially healthy is to create a personal money management system.

Think of this as you do your laundry system. Or your skin care routine. Or your housekeeping strategy. Insert your system of choice here. We have systems we follow because they produce the results we want. Your system includes the steps you take and the tools you use to get the job done. I'm nearly certain your systems are not exactly like mine, but in the end, we both get results that satisfy us.

Here's my laundry system. I start by sorting whites from colored items. I make my own laundry detergent (and I'll put it up against any commercial brand any day because it is that awesome . . . and for less than a nickel per load, it is also cheap), use an equally cheap laundry stain product called Soilove, do not use any softening products, and am a stickler for hot water for whites. See? I have a system.

Without a good money management system, you'll still be procrastinating about saving for retirement decades from now. You are about to learn just how important this is by the length and detail in this chapter. Please do not skip past it, even if you're certain you have a system that's working just fine. It may be. But let's find out for sure.

Perhaps you know what it feels like to have money control you. I do. I was forever overspending to the point of nervously waiting for the next month's income to cover this month's bills. I believed that more money would fix everything, but in the end, I learned that more was never enough. I changed, and so can you if you are willing to step up and assume the position of money manager.

You must begin to see yourself as the gatekeeper of your money and financial resources. It's a big responsibility. Nothing comes in or goes out without your knowledge and approval. You assign every dollar a job by telling it where to go and what to do. Then you make sure those dollars behave exactly as instructed.

Technology has transformed the process of money management from time-consuming drudgery to sleek and simple. I want to show you a basic system that relies on the technology available to anyone with a computer and internet access.

This system works for me. If you do not already have a system that is working well, I invite you to adopt mine. You may need to customize and tweak it a bit to make it your own, but it's a great starting place.

Your Tools

Here are five specific tools you need in your money manager tool belt.

1. Free checking account
2. Overdraft protection
3. Online savings account
4. System automation
5. Management software

Free Checking Account

Depending on where you bank, getting this essential tool into your tool belt may be as easy as fine-tuning the account you have. However, if you do not trust your bank, are being deluged with sneaky fees, and are forced to put up with pathetic customer service, it may be time to make a change. I'll tell you right up front that I am not a fan of big banks because of all the fees they charge and the lousy customer service they get away with. Take a look at your bank statement and you may see what I'm talking about. There are still good banks out there, but typically they're local independent banks, credit unions, or online banks.

Do not take this as a blanket recommendation to break up with your bank. First, you need to assess what you have before you make a decision to leave.

Here are the features you want in a checking account:

- A free account, which means no fees at all and no minimum balance requirements—in a real bank that is FDIC insured or NCUA insured in the case of a credit union.

- Unlimited internet access to your account via the bank's secure and encrypted website so you can see your balances and recent transactions.
- Free online bill pay that you can access anytime day or night.
- An account that can be linked electronically to other accounts such as savings and credit card accounts so you can easily transfer money from one account to another in a hurry.
- Great customer service in which you can speak with a live person.

Most banks and credit unions are up to speed with technology and allow online access. However, finding a free account may not be so easy. By free I mean, well . . . free! No fees, no charges, no minimum balance requirements. Why should you pay a dime to a bank for the privilege of having access to your own money? You shouldn't, and you don't have to. But it may require diligence on your part to find a truly free account.

The following banks offer free checking accounts that I believe are worth your consideration if you decide you need to make a change. Two of the banks offer both brick-and-mortar locations as well as online banking, and one is an online-only bank.

Charles Schwab Bank. With limited branch locations in only three states, Charles Schwab Bank offers what may be the only perfect free checking account on the planet, the Schwab Bank High Yield Investor Checking.[1] This is available online no matter where you live. It's such a great account and so easily accessed online that you may never have to go into a bank again. And it's free. It even offers a couple of things I've not seen at any other bank: no-fee overdraft protection and unlimited ATM reimbursements. Okay, some banks offer ATM reimbursements, but I have not found another one with unlimited reimbursements. This means you can use any ATM in the world and assume as many transaction fees as you want, and at the end of the month, you will be reimbursed for every fee. That's a huge benefit.

This free checking account pays variable interest on any balance and offers free online bill pay, mobile deposits, free standard checks, free prepaid deposit envelopes, and a Visa Platinum debit card. And there is one more totally awesome feature: excellent customer service. These people make you feel as though you are their best friend. I prefer online chat, which is very simple and user-friendly, but you can also call to speak with a human or interact by email.

Although opening this account will automatically open a linked brokerage account, don't worry. It also has no fees or minimums. And it can sit there completely inactive until such time that you might want to use it. In fact, until right now, I'd completely forgotten that I have an empty brokerage account with Schwab. This is truly an awesome free checking account.

USAA Bank. With limited locations in the San Antonio, Texas, area, USAA bank is an excellent organization offering online banking to anyone, anywhere. The free checking account[2] is truly free, with no maintenance fees, free online bill pay, free checks, prepaid envelopes to send in deposits, a free MasterCard debit card, and ATM reimbursements (not unlimited, however). Customer service is excellent, and a phone call will connect you to one of the lovely people who work at this fine organization.

Ally Bank. This is a "direct" or online bank, which means you access your checking account online, with mobile banking, by phone, or by ATM. Ally offers a free checking account[3] that meets my criteria: no minimum deposit requirements, no monthly maintenance fees, free bill pay and online banking, free MasterCard debit card, variable interest on balances, free checks, unlimited check writing, free balance alerts, and good customer service with the online chat option. Am I the only one who loves online chat? Maybe that's because I type faster than I talk, and I talk pretty fast.

Overdraft Protection

This is a must-have tool for your financial tool belt. Think of it as you would accident insurance. You have it then hope you'll never need it.

If you are an "overdrafter" (oh, how I can identify), it has to stop. There are few things as expensive and completely uncalled for as running up a pile of overdraft charges. For the person who is so out of touch with her current bank balance as to keep writing checks and swiping the debit card even when that balance has dropped to zero, overdrafting is very expensive. It's like pushing over the first domino.

Lisa, who wrote to me in complete desperation, admitted to having paid $1,400 in overdraft fees in a single year. That's more than an occasional flub. Lisa is a habitual overdrafter and has had more than a few bank accounts closed because of it. I would tell you what I told her: Stop it. Get a calculator and just stop it!

Overdrafting is serious, especially if you were to do this with, say, your mortgage payment. You need this kind of insurance in case it happens because of circumstances out of your control. (Lisa's were not.)

Overdraft protection is accomplished by instructing your bank to link your checking account to your savings, money market, or credit card account (or in the case of the Schwab account, your brokerage account), in which you have deposited some cash or have a line of credit. Then, if you make a mistake and overdraft your account, the bank will simply dip into your linked account to grab the necessary funds. They will charge you a $5 or $10 fee (except in the case of Schwab, which has no-fee overdraft protection), plus an annual fee of $25 to $50. But that's not as bad as the $35 you will be charged each time if you do not have overdraft protection, plus other charges, including in some cases $5 to $7 per day that your account remains in a negative condition.

If your overdraft protection comes from a line of credit or a credit card, using it will trigger an instant loan, and you'll be charged an extremely high interest rate on that loan. But if you pay it off quickly, it is usually much less costly than bouncing a check with no protection.

Do not confuse "overdraft protection" (a good thing) with "bounce protection" (a bad thing), which most banks and credit unions add automatically to checking accounts. They do this because bounce protection boosts the bank's profit margins. Let me be very clear: You do not want bounce protection. Here's how it works. If you do not have overdraft protection in place and you write a check or swipe your debit card for an amount that is greater than your current balance, the bank automatically lends you some of its money and charges very hefty fees on top of outrageous interest.

Banks love bounce protection because it feeds their bottom line. Unless you know for certain that you have overdraft protection, it is likely that you've agreed to bounce protection by default. Call right away to find out for sure what you have. If it's bounce protection, opt out and add overdraft protection. If you don't want overdraft protection, still opt out of bounce protection. But be aware that should you write a check or swipe your debit card for more than is in your account, the payment or charge will be denied, and you'll be hit with a hefty nonsufficient funds fee when your mortgage company or landlord is unable to cash your check.

Online Savings Account

The next tool you need for your tool belt is a savings account that pays a higher rate of interest than you'll find in a big bank, a local bank, or even a credit union. Online banks, because they are branch-free and spend very little on marketing, routinely pay interest rates that are from six to ten times more than banks and credit unions offer. Granted, at this time, even ten times the big bank interest on savings is quite low. Still, it's all relative.

You want an online savings account that has no minimum requirements, charges no fees, and links to your checking account electronically, no matter where that checking account may be. This means that with only a couple of clicks of your computer mouse you can transfer money between accounts freely and easily. This savings account will also be key to your money management system because it offers a great way to organize your money so you can keep track of exactly where it is and what it is doing.

The ideal high-yield savings account has an additional feature that is very useful—the ability to create sub-accounts within a single savings account. Creating sub-accounts is a great way to save for specific goals and manage your budget better. And you can visually see how your money is growing. That's the emotional payoff we all need.

There is one possible downside to having an online savings account (although I see it as more of a safety valve against hasty, irrational withdrawals): It can take a few business days to access the money in your account.

Typically, if you want to withdraw from your savings account, you log into your online savings account, initiate a free transfer to your checking account, and then wait three to five days for it to happen. If you need your money immediately, this could cause a problem. But this feature protects you—from you. You'll have at least three days to rethink whatever has prompted you to make this withdrawal.

While an online savings account at any of the online banks such as HSBCDirect, EmigrantDirect, and Ally will do a good job for you, I have a few recommendations for an online high-yield savings account that has superior features.

SmartyPig. This is not a bank per se, but all deposits are fully FDIC insured and earn one of the most competitive interest rates in the United States. This is a very unique and lovely website brought to you by an organization with a sterling reputation.[4] I would not hesitate one moment to put my money here. At SmartyPig, you open an account and then set up as many sub-accounts as you like, giving each one a savings goal. There are no fees and no minimum balance requirements. And I really like the encouragement and positive synergy going on at SmartyPig. You will find plenty of success stories about people who have developed a serious supersaver mentality.

The reason people are drawn to SmartyPig is to save money for a specific goal. But in truth, this is an insured savings account that earns the very best rate of interest available any-where. You can link your SmartyPig account to your check-ing account for ease of electronic transfers. And there is no limit to how much you can save. This is the real deal and an account you should consider seriously.

Capital One 360. Formerly ING Direct, this was the orig-inal online savings account[5] and still includes my favorite perk: You can split your account into sub-accounts, give them names such as "vacation" and "new car," and transfer money to them automatically. This is a great option for the highly organized saver.

System Automation

Technology offers you the ability to automate a great deal of your money management, and that is a very good thing. The more you can automate—set things up to happen auto-matically—the better manager you'll be. Automation is like delegating work to trusted staff members. That's what good managers, and smart women, do.

Automating is important because it removes that monthly decision making. You know, the decision of "Should I put money into building my emergency fund or buy that new sofa that is on sale for 50 percent off?" "Should I put twenty dollars into the Christmas fund or go out to lunch?" When decisions like that are put on autopilot, you will not even think about them. What you don't see, you will forget about. What you don't see, you don't miss.

Consider, for example, your regular contributions to the US Social Security Administration every payday, also known as FICA. Do you think about it? Miss that money? Change your mind from time to time about whether to contribute? No.

You don't lose a single moment of sleep over FICA! That's because it is automated. It is out of your control. Like it or not, you have to do it. End of story.

Automation brings psychological strength to the plans you make for your money. Do the work of automating your finances when you are in your most determined retirement-saving mood. You'll be thrilled with the results in years to come.

Online bill pay. Paper checks delivered via mail to pay one's bills are quickly going the way of the dinosaurs. A much more efficient and even safer way to send money to your creditors and service providers is by electronic transaction. Basically, you transfer the money out of your account into the account of the person you are paying. You skip all the paper—the payment stub, envelope, and postage stamp. Plus, with each transaction, you're creating a clear electronic history of the payment, no manila file folders and filing cabinets required. Transactions are all encrypted, which means they are safe from hackers and information thieves. What's more, you can see exactly when the payment is received.

Most banks and credit unions offer a free bill payment system for their checking account holders. If you've never taken advantage of this feature, you need to give it a try. Once you sign up for online bill pay, you will have the option to set up recurring payments (for something like your monthly mortgage or car payment). You input the amount and the day it is to be paid, and then you can forget about it. Your payments will go out exactly as you instruct. You can also make manual payments online for bills that vary in amount and frequency.

While most companies and service providers now accept electronic payments, if you want to send a payment to someone who doesn't, most banks (check with yours) will generate and mail the check as you instruct and even pay the postage. Again, you will have an electronic record to verify when the payment was sent and when the check cleared your account.

Automatic debits. This works the opposite of auto bill pay in that you authorize your service providers, such as utility companies, insurance companies, and others you select, to reach into your bank account and take the amount you owe automatically. Some lenders, such as those for student loans and mortgages, give a break on the interest rate when you set up your payments to be made automatically. That's a deal you should accept if offered. Go to your service providers' websites to see if they offer this service. Then take a deep breath and take the plunge. You'll enjoy the simplicity and peace of mind.

You can also set up auto debit with your credit card issuer to make sure you are never late with a payment. Here is how it works. You authorize your credit card company to automatically debit the minimum monthly payment due from your checking account before the due date. Now, even though you always pay your balance in full each month (You do, don't you? And even if you don't, please do this), you can relax, knowing the required payment has been made on time. You will never be late again. You can pay the rest when you get the statement. It's an added precaution that will make your life easier.

Automatic bill payment is a terrific way to make sure you don't accidentally miss a payment because it got lost in the mail, it fell behind the desk, or you just plain forgot because you were on vacation.

Direct deposits. If you haven't done so already, sign up to have your paychecks directly deposited into your checking account instead of dealing with a paper paycheck. This way the money is there at the same time every pay period and you don't have to fill out a deposit slip and either drive it to the bank or depend on the mail to get it there. Do the same for any other payments or income you receive. Call your company's human resources department or speak with your supervisor to find out how to set this up. If your company is quite small, you may not have this option.

You will discover other ways to automate your money management as you get into it. Many churches now offer automation for your giving. That may strike you as crass at first, but when you think about it, it's a good thing. You won't have to remember to bring your offering on Sunday, you'll be more faithful with giving (you'll give even when you aren't at church on a given Sunday), and you will have an accurate history when it comes time to file your tax returns.

Management Software

The last tool in your money management tool belt needs to be some kind of software that links all of your accounts together and keeps track of your spending so you know where you stand at all times. You have quite a few options, but here are my favorites.

Mvelopes. I am fond of this software because it is based on the old envelope budget system in which you take a stack of envelopes, write different categories on the outside (one for groceries, another for preschool tuition, another for gasoline, and so on), cash your paycheck, and divvy up the cash accordingly. When the cash is gone from an envelope, you stop spending until the next payday. Manual envelope budgeting works well, but it's archaic. I don't want to get stuck in the

1970s, and I'm sure you don't either. The modern method is Mvelopes.[6]

Once you set up your account, you can plan your spending by divvying up your paycheck into electronic "envelopes." I love this software because of this true budgeting feature. Other programs allow you to track what you've done but not actually plan what you will do. A basic Mvelopes account is free. A premium account that gives the kind of options you will eventually need is about $8 per month. Only you can decide if it's worth the price.

Mint. This website allows you to link all of your accounts and then keep track of all your activities. With a Mint account, you can track your spending, keep an eye on your goals, see how your investments are performing, and figure out where you can save money. All Mint accounts are free.[7]

Whatever you choose, make sure it works for you. The right budgeting software will make all the difference in helping you become a stellar money manager.

Putting It All Together

Once you have all of your management tools in place, make sure to link your online savings account to your checking account. You do this by going to your online savings account, looking for the prompts that allow you to identify the bank where your checking account is, and giving permission for the two to be linked. While you're there, check to make sure you know how to move funds electronically from checking into savings.

Create your savings sub-accounts and give each a nickname that tells you immediately what it's for (more on this in the coming chapters). This is simple if you have a Capital One

360 or SmartyPig account. If you have an online savings account that does not allow sub-accounts, open multiple savings accounts and name them accordingly. This is allowed.

Make sure you have arranged to have all of your paychecks and other sources of income deposited directly into your free checking account. Access your online bill paying feature on the bank's website (look for a link on the home page or bookmark it so you can go there directly). Set this up for your secure checking account, identifying the payees you will be sending money to most often and creating your unique address book. Make sure you know all the rules and how this works. It's not difficult, so just stay with it.

Go to the websites of your utility providers (power, water, cable, gas, internet, and so forth). Set up your accounts to allow for automatic debit to pay your bills. You should be able to pick a due date that works best with your management system. You may not want all of your bills coming due on the same day. Or you may prefer it that way. You're the boss, so you decide how you want this to work.

Spend time automating everything possible. Set alerts and arrange for balance notifications. If you have a smart mobile device, you will want to download an app that allows you to access your accounts on the go.

Set up your management software at Mvelopes, Mint, or use the software of your choice. Link all of your accounts, then become familiar with how the software operates. Learn how to create your spending plan and how to track your spending.

In the end it's not going to matter one whit how much money you made. It's what you did with it that will make all the difference. Having a great money management system that works for you and on which you know you can rely is the way to take responsibility for what you do with your money.

5

Put Your
Money Management
System to Work

Clarity about your money is essential. You need to know where it's going before you can even begin to make effective changes. That may sound obvious, but it's not. Beyond the rent and a close guess on utilities, most people cannot tell you how much they spend each month, or on what.

Jerrold Mundis

Anyone can set up an amazing money management system. Making it work is quite another thing. This requires commitment and technique.

If you are used to managing your income with a budget or spending plan, kicking it up a few notches now to get your retirement planning in order will not be a difficult adjustment.

But if you have a management style like the one I lived by for so many years in which you spend money until it's gone then white-knuckle it until you can manage to get more, you need a change. Your system does not work. Have you noticed this?

The 10-10-80 Solution

I love the "formula method" of money management. The one that has always worked for me is 10-10-80: save 10 percent, give 10 percent, and live on 80 percent.

Let that sink in for a moment.

Are you doing that now? If not, could you live on 80 percent of your income? It's easy to get sucked into a lifestyle that requires 100 percent or more of a family's income, leaving no room for saving or giving. And that's a problem. It's called living beyond your means. Nothing good can come from this. But do not worry about that right now. There are many ways to get your expenses down so they fit within 80 percent of your income. For more than twenty years I've been sharing thousands of little ways to cut expenses with my readers in my books like *Cheaper, Better, Faster* and at DebtProofLiving .com and EverydayCheapskate.com. Grab some coffee when you stop by to visit because you're going to start reading and find you just can't stop.

As for the first 10 percent, the rule is that you always save 10 percent of everything you receive. Always. If you start doing that at the beginning of your career, following the model I have taught for more than two decades at DebtProofLiving .com and in my related books, that money will build a killer emergency fund, possibly pay off your mortgage, and build wealth via investments and hard assets. When you make saving a habit, you'll never be broke.

The 60 Percent Solution

Another formula for your consideration was developed by Richard Jenkins at MSN Money and has come to be known as the 60 percent solution.

You begin by looking at the amount of income you bring in. You can look at it yearly, but it may be easier for you to implement and understand this plan if you look at it monthly or per pay period. Once you know your income, you follow the plan by keeping your expenses down to just 60 percent of your income. Your expenses include everything from your house payment to day care, from gas for your vehicle to insurance. Everything. These are all the things for which you are responsible. You have only 60 percent of your net income with which to pay for them, so it is time to take a good, hard look to see whether this is possible. If it is, you have made the first adjustment to becoming a more diligent saver. If it isn't, it may be time to take a look at the expenses you are responsible for to see what is pushing you over the limit.

For many people, their mortgage payment or car payment is eating up too much of their 60 percent. If this is true for you, consider making a change to something that is more affordable. Some people look at the figures and notice that their credit card payments are pushing them over the 60 percent limit. It may be that you tend to overspend on things that aren't necessary. It could be the constant eating out and entertainment every month. It could be clothing, furniture, or household items that are weighing you down. Look for places to cut that will keep you within the 60 percent solution.

So what happens to the 40 percent that remains? This portion of your net income is what you save, according to

Jenkins's plan. Yes, it is a lot. Yes, it may seem unattainable. However, you can divide up the 40 percent to put it in perspective.

Use 10 percent for retirement savings. Invest 10 percent, looking for some type of return. Ten percent should be saved in an easily accessible account for emergencies, recommends Jenkins. Finally, the last 10 percent is for yourself. Use it throughout the month for fun things you and your family want to do, or save that 10 percent for a future vacation. In either case, this 10 percent is yours.

At first, this might seem like an impossible plan. But instead of wasting time with specific budgets that just don't seem manageable, you may find that the 60 percent solution makes it easy to stay within your limits and save up for various things, giving you the feeling of real success.

The 50 Percent Solution

Elizabeth Warren, Harvard Law School professor, gets even stricter in the book she co-wrote with her daughter titled *All Your Worth*.[1] She says that to build your lifetime money plan you need to start with what's most important—your basic necessities. These are the must-have bills—those you need to pay month in and month out, no matter what. They include your rent or mortgage payment, utilities, insurance, car payment, regular medical bills, and any legal obligations (such as student loans). If you pay for day care so you can work, this is also a must-have bill. The list also includes a basic food allowance (just the bare essentials—T-bone steaks and restaurant meals don't qualify as must-have bills). Add up all these regular expenses and call the list your "Monthly Must-Have Expenses."

According to Warren, you should be able to cover your monthly must-have expenses on 50 percent of your take-home income. That's right—half of your money can go to must-haves. If you keep your must-haves to 50 percent of your income, you will have plenty left over to spend and to save for your future. Keeping the must-have expenses in balance will give you a solid foundation for your lifetime money plan.

What if you can't manage your bills on 50 percent of your income? This is a strong sign that it is time to cut back. Maybe you should send back the rent-to-own television. Maybe it is time to move to a smaller apartment or to trade in the car for something cheaper. Maybe you need to share expenses with a roommate or a family member. Do whatever you can to get your basic expenses down to half of your income. These can be tough choices, but in the long run, you'll live happier and rest easier if you start to get your budget straight now.

Money Rules

Whatever way you decide to divvy up your household income, you can see that you need a technique that works well for you.

In addition, I have developed a personal set of money rules that keep me on track. They're like guardrails that keep me from veering off into oncoming traffic or off the side of a cliff, metaphorically speaking. These rules work for me, and I hope they will work for you too.

You can find a much more complete treatment of the seven rules in my book 7 *Money Rules for Life*. In the meantime, here is an overview of these simple but effective money rules for managing your personal finances.

1. *Spend less than you earn*. So simple but not always understood. Spending less than you earn is not the same as

not spending more than you earn. Spending less results in a gap between the amount you earn and what you spend every month. That gap is important, because as you widen the gap, you will increase your options and financial freedom.

2. *Save some.* Out of every paycheck and every other source of personal income, take 10 percent right off the top and save it. This is a hard-and-fast rule, and you will learn what to do with this pool of money in future chapters.

3. *Give some.* Giving away some of your money out of gratitude for all you have is not only honoring to God, who is the source, but also quiets fear and greed. Giving says, "I may not have it all, but I do have enough, and I am grateful."

4. *Anticipate irregular expenses.* Not all of your expenses occur routinely every month. Take vacations, holiday spending, and car repairs, for example. If you do not anticipate these irregular expenses, they will catch you off guard and send your finances reeling. You'll be headed for the credit cards every time. You can anticipate these expenses by saving a little each month in a designated account where the money will accumulate until you need it.

5. *Tell your money where to go.* You know the word I'm about to utter, so brace yourself. It's coming. I cannot sugarcoat this. The only way you can effectively take control of your money is with a *budget.* You can also call it a *spending plan.* If you do not have one, you need one, starting today.

6. *Manage your credit.* Maintaining a great credit score means keeping a clean record. No one else in the world cares one whit about your credit report. You have to become your own credit report and credit score manager. Simple steps will keep you in charge and your three-digit score in fine shape.

1. Pay your bills on time every time. Never be late.

2. Order and review each of your three credit reports every twelve months. They are free at annualcreditreport .com. Dispute anything you do not know to be true.

3. Add up all of the credit limits on your credit card accounts. Now add up all of your owing debt on those cards. That total should never be more than 30 percent of the total credit limits. Keep it at or below that level. Zero percent (meaning that you have $0 balance on every card) is your goal.

4. Do not apply for new credit. Close old lines of credit systematically, no more than one every six months. Opening new and closing old lines of credit will both put dings in your credit score.

7. *Borrow only what you know you can repay.* The only way you can know for sure that you have the money to repay a debt is to have the money! But why would you borrow money if you have the money? Good question. Having the money means you have the resources available to repay the debt. That means the debt needs to be secured or collateralized. You have the money to repay your home mortgage in the property itself. You could sell the house and repay the debt. Other guidelines apply to other types of loans such as student loans and car loans.

You should borrow no more in student loans than is equal to the first year's income on the job for which you are preparing. Example: If you are going to be a first-grade teacher in a district where first-time teachers earn $27,000 annually, your entire college career should produce no more than $27,000 in student debt. Of course, less would be so much better. And when it comes to automobile loans, never finance a car over more than 36 months. Statistically, after a car reaches age three, it begins to need maintenance. You don't want payments and repair bills at the same time.

Now that you have your tools in place, I recommend you deposit all of your income into your free checking account. But don't dump and run. It should take only a few minutes a month to manage that money. Leave the amount you need to pay your current bills in the account. That may be 50 or 60 percent, maybe more, perhaps less. Then see that the balance is immediately transferred to the appropriate savings sub-accounts.

Figure Out Where You Are

Do you know that feeling of being lost—you know, like in the woods or even in a mall? You're confused, and you don't know which way to turn to get back on track. And then you spot a map with a big red dot that says, "You are here." Rescued! Even if you've veered off course and taken a tragic detour, as long as you know where you are, you can figure out how to get to your destination. The same thing is true with managing your money. Before you can do anything, you need to figure out where you are—you need to figure out your true expenses.

The only way to know for sure what your monthly needs are is to start tracking your expenses. Keep a journal and record every dime you spend, and I mean all of it. You and your spouse both need to do this to get an adequate picture, and you need to do this for at least thirty days.

Not every month is the same (you have expenses that are irregular, such as car maintenance; some that are unexpected, such as an emergency trip to the dentist; and some that are intermittent, such as clothing and gifts), but once you've tracked your spending for thirty days, you'll be able to estimate and project expenses that do not recur every month.

Once you have a good idea of your average monthly expenses, determine what they are in relationship to your income. Be honest. I know this can be shocking, but it's a reality you must face. If you need 90 percent or even more of your take-home pay just to get by each month, this is not good.

Managing money responsibly is a learned skill. However, I do believe some of us were born with temperaments that make it somewhat more challenging, while some were born with a natural bent toward money management. Let me encourage you again by saying that if I can learn to do this, I have no doubt you can too. More than that, I have even gone on to make financial literacy an important part of my everyday life, which keeps me on track and moving forward rather than sliding back down the mountain into my old way of life. Take the time and effort to learn financial management skills, and they will help you become a trustworthy steward.

6

Build an Emergency Fund

This is perhaps the main lesson of this whole experience. It is basic but still unlearned: human beings must have savings. This is not just a good idea. It's the difference between life and death, terror and calm. So start saving right now, and don't stop until you die.

Ben Stein

An emergency fund is the most important factor in your retirement savings. "What?!" I can hear you asking. "More important than my 401(k)? Or paying off my home?" Yes, and there are a couple of reasons why.

An emergency fund is like the starter on an automobile. If you can't get a car started, what good is it? It doesn't matter what kind of engine the car has or how completely awesome the transmission or fuel economy system. It doesn't matter how gorgeous the interior or flawless the paint job. If it won't start, what good is it? It might look good sitting in the driveway, but that's a pretty expensive piece of yard art.

An emergency fund also has a kind of psychological effect that makes you feel safe and protected from danger. Think of seat belts, oat bran, and guardrails. Or better yet, a massive, sturdy wall between you and financial devastation.

Life is not always predictable, as I'm sure you've noticed. If you are not well prepared to handle your short-term financial emergencies, that's a good indicator you're living on the edge, spending all you have and most likely relying on credit cards to bail you out. Then the resulting higher monthly credit card payments put you farther and farther from a place where you can get serious about saving for retirement. It's a vicious circle, and if you don't do something drastic to stop the momentum, you'll be on the credit card treadmill forever. And I'm talking about into retirement and beyond.

I am going to go even further and predict that without a solid, respectable emergency fund, you will never be in a position to fund your 401(k) or other type of retirement savings account, nor will you ever pay off your home. An emergency fund is that important to your life because as it grows, it holds your financial foundation firm against the strong currents that could so easily wash you out to sea.

A Contingency Fund

While *emergency fund* is a generic term also known as a nest egg or rainy-day fund, at Debt-Proof Living this is known as a Contingency Fund. Creating a Contingency Fund is as simple and informal as taking a dollar, putting it into an envelope, and writing "Contingency Fund" on the front, then adding another dollar, and a five, and coming up with creative ways to spend less to have more to add to it until—and as soon as possible—you park this money in a place with the following criteria.

Safety. Your Contingency Fund needs to be safe from any kind of erosion. It should be in a risk-free savings account, not the stock market or any other kind of investment where you could lose any part or all of it. You also want it to be safe from you. This is why it needs to be in a bank or credit union or some other kind of guaranteed safe account—not in your top drawer or under the mattress.

Liquidity. This money needs to be available to you within two or three days at the most if and when you need it. This too precludes putting the money into an investment or a certificate of deposit, lending it to a friend, or, in a moment of weakness, lending it to yourself. Money that is lent or invested is not considered liquid.

Growth. Believe it or not, the least important factor in deciding on the best place for your Contingency Fund is the interest it will earn. Once you have determined the safe place that has no restrictions or conditions concerning access to your money, then you want to think about the best interest rate you can find. Best case scenario is that you will not need your Contingency Fund for a long time, so you want to earn at least enough interest to stay ahead of inflation. Your online savings account, which is attached to your checking account, is the ideal place to park your Contingency Fund because it meets all of the criteria.

How much to save. When you lose your job or experience some other event that compromises your income, statistics suggest the condition will continue for three to six months. It could be less time, but it also could be more. Your goal is to accumulate and maintain enough money in your Contingency

Fund to pay all of your essential living expenses during that period of time. My advice is that your goal should be to have six months of expenses tucked away in this fund.

To determine your Contingency Fund goal, estimate what your bare-bones requirements will be while you are without income. Keep in mind that should you lose your income and need to turn to your Contingency Fund, you will be replacing your take-home not your gross income. Also, you will be going into essentials-only mode. You will more than likely cease all optional spending. My point is that the cost of your essential needs during your incomeless time may be considerably less than your current gross income.

Let's say your gross household income is $6,000 a month. However, by the time you allow for taxes and other deductions plus work-related expenses you would not have during a time of unemployment, you could probably squeak by on $4,200. In this example, your Contingency Fund goal should be $4,200 times three, or $12,600. Multiply by six to get the optimum savings goal of $25,200. Shocked? Take a deep breath and slowly exhale. Reality can be daunting, especially if you, like the majority of Americans, have something like $13.27 in savings.

How to Manage a Contingency Fund

Managing a Contingency Fund is the easy part. Just get started and keep making deposits regularly and routinely every time you receive your income. And as far as humanly possible, try to forget about any withdrawal options.

Following the 10-10-80 formula, 10 percent of whatever you deposit into your checking account should be immediately transferred into your Contingency Fund sub-account until you reach your goal. By transferring it right away, it's one level removed from your access. Those dollars have been told what to do and sent away to get their job done. They are no longer available for spending.

Once your Contingency Fund is fully funded, you don't stop saving. Instead, you stop adding to this fund and redirect your regular savings elsewhere (more on this in coming chapters).

The way to manage your Contingency Fund is to feed it regularly and not touch it unless it is a true emergency. The Nordstrom semiannual sale is not an emergency, nor is a summer vacation or your daughter's wedding. To be considered a true emergency, it needs to rise to the level of being a threat to your physical or financial well-being.

The purpose of your Contingency Fund is to keep you afloat during those times that your income stream dries up. We're talking serious stuff, such as unemployment, medical emergencies, and big financial needs that if not covered by your Contingency Fund are sure to put you into a serious financial tailspin and send you running for a credit card bailout. Your Contingency Fund is for serious, short-term needs.

If and when the time comes that you need to call your Contingency Fund into action, you will do so with mixed emotions. On the one hand, you'll be grateful that you don't have to worry about living off your credit cards because you are able to fund your own emergencies. But on the other hand, you will remember how hard you worked to build it. Don't be surprised when you are very reluctant to use it. In fact, when it comes right down to using your Contingency Fund to live on, you will likely find you have the ability to be more frugal than you ever dreamed possible.

Once you are back on your feet, you must make it a top priority to restore your Contingency Fund to its goal as quickly as possible. The way to do this is the same way you built your Contingency Fund in the first place—with the 10 percent you are saving every month. Once you are back to your goal, you can move on, knowing you covered that emergency without creating new debt.

Speaking of goals, yours will change with time. Take a couple of seconds to ponder what it cost you to pay all of your bills and keep body and soul together ten years ago when you were single or when you were newly married and could live on a buck thirty-five a day. A little less than it costs today, right? And things will be more expensive and your life will change dramatically over the coming ten years.

Your lifestyle is bound to become more costly as things become more expensive over time. Add to that the ways your income increases, which usually prompts changes in lifestyle as the years roll by. You may move to a larger home, add children, build assets, grow wealth, and so on.

You will need to reassess what six months' of living expenses look like from time to time, making sure your Contingency Fund reflects these changes. This is good money management.

Many benefits, both financial and emotional, come with a Contingency Fund. The act of saving alone brings a certain sense of calm. It puts a lid on discontentment, greed, and self-pity. Dealing with life as it happens is a lot easier when you take away the sense of panic.

Questions and Answers

As you can imagine, I've received many questions related to creating and growing a Contingency Fund. These represent those asked most often.

Q: I am so depressed. There is no way we will ever be able to save $10,000, $25,000, or even $100, to be perfectly honest. Don't you understand that in my situation this is completely impossible?

A: Your reaction is understandable and more common than you might think. If you've never had a specific savings plan, this is overwhelming. Here's a way to break this down into something more bite-size.

How much would it take for you to get through just one week if you lost your household income? Think groceries, gasoline, one-fourth of your rent, etc. $500? $700? Whatever it is, make that your first goal. When you reach it, go for two weeks. Then one month, and on and on. This will require sacrifice for a time, but I know you can do this. That's because I know the power of a smart woman committed to a cause.

What if the doctor told you that your precious daughter has a medical condition that can only be treated with medication that costs $2,000 each month for one year? Insurance will not pay for it, and you must come up with that amount in cash to save her life. Would you throw up your hands and say you cannot afford it? Would you whine and mope while still eating out three times a week, getting regular manicures, and insisting you cannot live without your smartphone and pricey data plan? Not a chance. You would stop at nothing to raise those funds to save your daughter's life. I know it. You have to see getting control of your money, starting with your Contingency Fund, as a kind of life-and-death matter. It is that important.

Start today. Get serious. Expand your view beyond the new outfit you just have to get so you can see a larger view of the future. Find ways to raise cash, such as selling things you don't use and don't need. Cancel the cable TV. Drop your data plan in favor of a bare-bones, prepaid mobile phone. There are many ways you can cut your expenses to have the money you need to save. Before you know it, you will have accumulated a sizable Contingency Fund, and you will be proud. Deservedly.

Q: Okay, let's say we get started. We're doing well and build the balance to $2,000. Then our van dies and requires repairs that are $1,800. So what do we do? Put that on a credit card while we have $2,000 in the bank?

A: You do raise a perplexing scenario. But let's look at this logically. This could be the first time you have options when it comes to dealing with an emergency, because you, like so many, have never saved in advance for things that are unexpected. You are doing great!

I would advise you to pay cash for your van's engine from your Contingency Fund. That qualifies as a fairly significant emergency. However, let's just say for a moment that you did put it on a credit card. Your new monthly payment on that amount would be at least $100. If going that route is a possible solution (I assume it would be, because if you had not saved the $2,000, you would surely see putting the cost on a credit card as your only option), then it only stands to reason you should be able to pay this amount to yourselves. Do you see where I'm going with this?

You are in effect making a loan to yourselves from your Contingency Fund. Treat it as such and sign a promissory note between you and the Bank of Us, agreeing to pay $100 a month over and above your regular deposit into your Contingency Fund. The great thing is that there is no interest involved here. You borrow $1,800 and you repay $1,800. And if eighteen months seems like a very long time, put your own feet to the fire and double those extra payments to $200. You'll have the amount paid off in nine months. With a credit card, it would be a much different story. If you paid off a balance of $1,800 at 16.9 percent interest using the minimum monthly payment option, it would take you sixteen years to repay that car repair bill. And in addition to paying back the $1,800, you would also pay $2,647 in interest. I'll bet you're liking the terms at the Bank of Us a lot better.

Q: I contribute 10 percent of my income to a 401(k) plan. Can't I count that as my Contingency Fund?

A: No, because it is not liquid. You could not get your hands on that money in a hurry. You shouldn't even think of that as your money for now. And taking a loan from it or cashing it in could result in huge penalties and tax consequences. However, you might want to consider discontinuing or reducing your 401(k) contributions for a while. That would allow you to build your Contingency Fund more quickly.

Q: Let's say I reach my goal and our Contingency Fund is fully funded. Can I stop saving 10 percent?

A: No. You will always save at least 10 percent forever, for the rest of your life. Funding your Contingency Fund is just the first level of a lifelong savings plan, which you will learn in the coming chapters.

7

Get Out of Debt

No investment is as secure as a repaid debt.

Austin Pryor

If you are carrying unsecured debt, it's killing you. I know a thing or two about this, and I'm talking in terms of stress, worry, and flat out cold cash. Those debts are stealing your future.

Every credit card debt, student loan, and personal loan with your name on it has a legal right to your future income. And we're not talking chump change. Your student debt could be costing you anywhere from 6 to 8 percent annually in interest alone, while credit cards these days are charging upwards of 29.99 percent. That's a hefty bite out of money you have not even earned yet.

If you've been wondering how on earth you will be able to fund your Contingency Fund (previous chapter) let alone contribute to retirement savings accounts (coming up) and personal savings and investments (ditto), this is one of the places to look. Add up your monthly unsecured debt payments. Now imagine if all of those debts were paid in full and you had that amount each month to prepare for emergencies and for retirement too.

But first let's define "unsecured debt." If whatever you bought on credit cannot be repossessed for failure to pay, it is an unsecured debt. Those really cute shoes? Bloomingdale's does not want them back and will not send out the shoe police to get them. Same for your education. Those semesters and even your awesome degree—paid for in part with student loans—cannot be rescinded if it turns out you are unable to pay the debt. You owe that money no matter what.

A secured debt, on the other hand, can be repossessed because there is collateral involved. Take your automobile, for example. If you have a loan payment each month, the car itself is the collateral or "security" for the lender. If you miss payments, the lender will arrange to have the car repossessed. Same with a home that is mortgaged. That mortgage is secured by the property or real estate. The legal documents you signed give the lender the right to seize the collateral for failure to pay.

Secured debt is somewhat "safer" than unsecured debt. With secured debt, there is a way out for both the lender and the borrower. The borrower can sell the collateral to pay the lender. Or the lender can take the collateral to satisfy the loan. It's this kind of safety valve that makes secured debt safer.

Unsecured debt, however, is dangerous, especially if it is subject to variable rates of interest the way most credit cards are these days. Think of the restaurant meals you've put on credit. Christmas gifts. Weekends away. They're over and done with, and all you have are the memories and the recurring debt payments. The answer, of course, is to pay off your unsecured debt as fast as possible. You will not be surprised to know I have a plan for you.

If you live debt-free and never pay interest, you can skip this chapter. But if you're paying interest on credit card accounts, college loans, or other unsecured debt, imagine all of those dollars going into your retirement savings instead of lining the pockets of your creditors.

It is possible for you to get out of debt. I've been helping people do that for more than twenty years through my organization Debt-Proof Living. I would love to lead you out of that financially debilitating way of life as well.

In a nutshell, here's how the Rapid Debt-Repayment Plan (RDRP) works. You pay off your loan with the shortest term first and then use the extra money to prepay other loans. It is a very simple concept, which is what makes it so exciting.

The key to turning the concept into action is to follow the simple RDRP rules and to create a chart that you can hang on your refrigerator that shows in black and white your detailed payment schedule right down to the final $0. Let me show you how this works.

You will base your RDRP on your current minimum monthly payments. It is not necessary to add any additional funds to the amounts you are paying right now. This is the beauty of the plan. It takes the very least amount you are required to pay this month, uses that figure to establish your base, and then turns it into your get-out-of-debt card.

This is a key point, and one that many people miss: You do not have a choice whether or not to pay your minimum monthly payments this month. Your RDRP is based on those minimum payments. Therefore, it is a plan you can and must put into effect immediately. It requires no new funding from you. It simply takes what you are already required to do and turns it into a plan that will effectively get you out of debt.

The RDRP is designed for your unsecured debt. That does not mean the concept will not work for auto loans, home equity loans, and even mortgages. However, I want to caution you not to include your secured debt in your initial RDRP. The focus of the RDRP as presented here is to rid you of the most egregious of your debts, which are your high-interest, unsecured consumer debts.

The Rapid Debt-Repayment Plan consists of five simple rules:

Rule 1: No more new debt. This means you must immediately stop adding any new purchases to any of your unsecured debts. You cannot put out a raging fire if you continue to pour gasoline on it. You cannot stop your bathtub from overflowing unless you turn off the tap. You cannot get out of debt unless you stop adding to it. If you do not stop incurring new debt, neither this plan nor any other plan will ever work for you. You will go to your grave in perma-debt, which is a depressing thought but something you need to consider.

Rule 2: Add up your current minimum payments. Make a list of the payments you must make for one month on your credit cards, store charge cards, installment loans, and personal loans. Include medical and dental payments, student loans—every unsecured debt for which you are currently responsible to make payments.

Rule 3: Arrange these debts according to the time it will take to pay them off. Developing your RDRP by hand using a financial calculator is not impossible, but it is tedious. This is why we created the RDRP Calculator® for members of Debt-ProofLiving.com. You simply input your current balances, interest rates, and current payments. One click produces your custom RDRP showing the exact month you will be debt-free.

Rule 4: Pay the same amount every month. Here is another way to put this: Fix your monthly payments. Do not pay attention to your creditors, who will say you can pay less each month, which is what we call the "falling payment" method. For example, if your payment this month to your VISA account is $43, that will be your monthly payment to that debt until it is paid in full, even though VISA will accept less as your balance declines. If the total of your debt payments this month is $320, rule 4 requires that you pay that same amount every month until you are debt-free.

Rule 5: As one debt is paid, add its payment to the regular payment of the next debt in line. This is where the rapid part comes in, because you are prepaying your debts with payments far greater than required. But still your total monthly debt payment remains the same. This is the key to getting out of debt fast.

Take a look at the RDRP example below. You see that by following the five simple RDRP rules, the entire debt is repaid in just eighteen months. According to the creditors' plans, paying off this same debt load would have taken more than twenty-two years.

If you are struggling with the idea of concentrating on the shortest debt first (not necessarily the one with the highest interest rate), understand that there's a good reason: You are going to need a big emotional payoff as quickly as possible. Reaching that first $0 will give you an emotional payoff like you never dreamed possible. You need a get-out-of-debt plan that works and one you will stick with. This is it. Believe me.

Rapid Debt-Repayment Plan

Debts are arranged in the order of the number of months required to pay them off with the shortest in the first position, not according to the interest rate or outstanding balance.

Wow! The first zero balance after only 3 months! Time for a small celebration.

MasterCard gets $145 this month, which is the regular $120 payment plus the $25 that went to JCPenney previously.

In month 11 the orthodontist receives his regular $80 payment plus $185, which used to go to JCPenney, MasterCard, and VISA, for a total of $265.

The total of the minimum monthly payments in the first month is $320. This becomes a fixed monthly expense and should be entered on the monthly spending plan.

Creditor	# Mos	$$ Bal	%	4/03 #1	5/03 #2	6/03 #3	7/03 #4	8/03 #5	9/03 #6	10/03 #7	11/03 #8	12/03 #9	1/04 #10	2/04 #11	3/04 #12	4/04 #13	5/04 #14	6/04 #15	7/04 #16	8/04 #17	9/04 #18	10/04 #19
JCPenney	3	71		25	25	23	0															
MasterCard	8	1,000		120	120	122	145	145	145	145	124	0										
VISA	10	498		40	40	40	40	40	40	40	61	185	12	0								
Orthodontist	15	1,850		80	80	80	80	80	80	80	80	80	253	265	265	265	265	104	0			
Discover	18	1,497		55	55	55	55	55	55	55	55	55	55	55	55	55	55	216	320	320	79	0
Totals		**4,916**		320	320	320	320	320	320	320	320	320	320	320	320	320	320	320	320	320	79	0

Debt-Free!

8

Maximize Your
Retirement Accounts

Do one thing every day that scares you.

Eleanor Roosevelt

Here's my promise. I will try to make this chapter as brief and enjoyable as possible. You need this information because there are several actions you must take. You do not have a choice. And there may be free money involved. No kidding. So here we go.

While retirement accounts have different names, the most common is 401(k). You probably have this option if you work. If you don't work, you still have options, which we'll cover in a bit.

Many women don't join their employer's payroll deduction retirement savings plans, be that plan a 401(k), a 403(b), or another tax-advantaged retirement account. Studies show that the nonparticipation rate runs between 25 and 33 percent of all employees.[1] That's a lot of people who are passing up a good thing.

Government-sanctioned retirement accounts, most often referred to as 401(k) accounts (they can have different designations, such as 403[b], IRA, Roth IRA, and so forth), are fairly recent, established in the United States in 1983. These accounts are all "tax-advantaged" because they allow the retirement saver (you) an advantage by either deferring or forgiving taxes you would otherwise have to pay if you took possession of the money first, paid the taxes, and then saved or invested for the future out of your after-tax dollars.

The most important thing you need to know about tax-advantaged retirement savings vehicles is that they are both government created and government controlled. Under these government-controlled plans, the federal government makes all the rules, both on the money going in and the money coming out. And they can change the rules on a dime and even make those changes retroactive.

With this in mind, let's look at an overview of the most common tax-advantaged retirement accounts.

Types of Accounts

401(k). Depending on the type of business (for-profit, nonprofit, self-employed, state-sponsored, governmental, etc.), the designation or name of the plan may vary, but the general rules apply. You contribute pretax dollars through your employer. The money is deducted from your paycheck, deposited into your retirement account, and invested in funds that you select from the menu provided by the plan administrator.

Many employers hand out "free money" to all who participate in their company's retirement savings plan to help their employees save for the future. Some employers give a lump sum each pay period to those who have opted into the plan, say 3 percent of your pay, even if you do not participate by contributing some of your own money. Others give dollar-for-dollar matches up to a set limit. I've heard of employers who give a lot, perhaps 10 percent of your pay, if you first contribute 2 percent, while others may offer some other kind of matching program.

If your employer offers any kind of incentive, how can you pass it up? To do so would be to leave free money sitting on the table. At the very least, as soon as you are eligible, you need to sign up to participate in your company's retirement savings plan at least up to the match. Even if you leave your job, the money you contributed is yours and all or part of the money your employer contributed may be yours, depending on the vesting rules of the company's plan. You can take your 401(k) and roll it over into an IRA or a Roth IRA. If you choose a Roth, you will have to pay taxes on the amount you're rolling over, as Roth IRAs use posttax money.

You will have a choice about how much of each paycheck will go into your account to be held for retirement. Someone who puts $4,000 a year into a retirement account starting at age twenty-two can have $1 million by age sixty-two, assuming 8 percent average annual returns. Wait ten years to start contributing, and you'd have to put in more than twice that amount—$8,800 a year—to reach the same goal.

One of the rules is that once money is deposited into your account, you are not allowed to take possession of or have access to the funds. The money is managed by a custodian. Your access is at arm's length until such time as you withdraw the funds and pay the taxes, which will be, at the earliest, age fifty-nine and a half. There are limits on how much you can contribute to an employer-sponsored retirement account plan, and these limits can change annually. For example, the contribution limit for 401(k) plans, 403(b) plans, and the federal government's Thrift Savings Plan increased from $17,000 in 2012 to $17,500 in 2013. However, the catch-up contribution limit for employees age fifty and older remained unchanged at $5,500. This means if you are fifty or over, in 2013 you can contribute an additional $5,500 to your account to make up for years you may not have contributed enough.

IRA. An Individual Retirement Account (IRA) is for any individual who has taxable compensation or self-employment income who will not reach age seventy and a half by the end of the year. In 2013, you are able to contribute $5,500 a year to an IRA, $6,500 if you are over fifty. All money contributed to an IRA, along with whatever it earns, goes untaxed as long as the money is in the IRA. You cannot set this up at work, but that's no problem. You can open an IRA at a bank or other financial services companies that have received IRS approval to offer IRAs.

Your contribution may be limited if you are covered by a retirement plan at work, so you will need to check on this when you open the account. Your contributions to your IRA account are tax deductible because rather than funding with pretax dollars, you do so with after-tax dollars.

Spousal IRA. Every spouse, with or without income, can open a Spousal IRA. The only requirement is that the working partner earns enough income to cover the contribution. As long as your husband earns $11,000 in income, he can put $5,500 into his IRA and $5,500 into yours each year. If you are fifty or older, you may each contribute $6,500. You can deduct the contributions on your tax return, following the rules and guidelines set up by the IRS.

Roth IRA. This is my personal retirement account of choice. It's like an IRA, in that you set it up on your own outside of your employment and make contributions on your own. The money you put into a Roth IRA is not deductible. You must contribute after-tax dollars—money that has already been taxed. That is the key. The payoff is that you never have to pay taxes on that money again or on its growth. No matter how much your money increases over the years, you will not pay taxes when you take it out, even if it is many years from now.

Roth IRAs, however, are not available to everybody; the IRS allows only people earning under a certain amount (which varies based on several factors) to contribute to Roth IRAs. For example, if you are married, filing jointly, and your modified adjusted gross income (AGI) is less than $178,000, both of you can contribute to an individual Roth IRA in 2013 up to $5,500 each. If you are single and your AGI is less than $112,000 in 2013, you can contribute $5,500 to a Roth IRA.[2] The IRA issues new contribution limits each year.

Spousal Roth IRA. The same terms and conditions apply as for the Spousal IRA above.

The Fine Print

There are rules. Lots of them. You cannot make a withdrawal before age fifty-nine and a half or you will suffer a significant penalty of 10 percent, plus state and federal taxes will become due on the entire amount. Please consult with your tax advisor on all of this. There are so many rules and conditions and they change so often that it is impossible for me to outline every one of them here. And they change every year, which is one more reason never to assume anything when it comes to retirement accounts. It's a good idea to regularly consult IRS Publication 590, which you can find at IRS.gov, for the most current restrictions, rules, and regulations regarding retirement accounts.

Anyone can open IRAs and Roth IRAs. However, income limitations will determine how much of your contribution is deductible and how much you can contribute.[3] Again, please contact your tax advisor for information that applies to your individual situation.

I would be remiss if I did not offer a word of caution on government-controlled retirement accounts. Because the government controls them, the government gets to make the rules. The rules can change. What if the federal government decided in, say, 2020 to help solve the Social Security crisis by placing a 40 percent surcharge on all withdrawals from 401(k)s and IRAs? Or what if the government announced that retroactively to January 1, 2010, all funds in retirement accounts are converted into US Treasury Bonds with a guaranteed 2 percent interest? Could they do it? Sure they could. And because that money has not been taxed, the account holders (you and I) would have no recourse.

There is, however, a plausible argument that these kinds of changes would not affect Roth IRAs. Because the account holder has already paid taxes on the amounts contributed (up to each year's limitation), those accounts would likely be treated differently. We cannot know for sure, but it makes sense to me.

Many financial advisors, including my own, consider the tax-deferral provided by plans such as the 401(k) and IRA to be a huge benefit to their clients. The logic goes something like this: Since you will be spending your entire working life in a higher tax bracket and will retire in a lower tax bracket, doesn't it make sense to delay the payment of taxes until you retire and are in a lower tax bracket? Many consider the tax deferral provided by the 401(k) and IRA to be the biggest benefit of tax-advantaged retirement accounts.

Fees Matter

There is something else you need to know about 401(k) employer-provided retirement accounts: fees. Horrendous fees! Until only recently, Congress has allowed plan providers to keep the fee structure on these accounts hidden from employers and account holders. How ridiculous is that! The word on the street is that the fees are so high that consumers would be outraged.[4] In fact, some surveys suggest that many account holders are unaware they are paying any fees at all.[5] But that is changing. Effective 2013, fees must be disclosed to every person who has a 401(k) or similar retirement account. This could get very interesting because the companies that manage these funds earn billions of dollars every year in fees alone.

Typically, fees are deducted right off the top of an account, and since there has been no requirement to disclose the amount, it's done quietly. If you have a retirement account already, you may not even be aware that you have been paying management fees for administrative costs, sales commissions, advertising, insurance, and all manner of expenses involved with running a business.

Let me show you an example of why fees matter when growing a retirement nest egg over one's working career. We'll use these terms: The employee contributes $5,000 per year for forty years at an average annual return of 7 percent. Consider the following amounts paid in fees:

Annual Fee	Total Amount
0.5%	$878,159
1%	773,809
2%	603,998
3%	475,127

Would you have imagined that the difference between .5 percent and 3 percent in management fees could mean more than $400,000 over the long haul?

Fees matter, and hopefully now that fees must be disclosed to account holders, those companies that manage retirement accounts will become more competitive to reduce the bite that management takes out of your nest egg.

None of this means I am suggesting you should not participate. Every woman, whether she works outside the home or works at home—or over the years does some of both—needs to have her own tax-advantaged retirement account. I want to show you a strategy that will allow you the most advantage, or the best of both worlds, with the least risk as you fund your retirement account.

Retirement Account Strategy

Unless you are independently wealthy, you should have both a Roth IRA and a 401(k). And you can, provided you don't exceed the income limits, which you can find at IRS.com when you search "IRA Contribution Limits."

At the beginning of each year, make certain you are contributing up to the match into your 401(k) plan, provided your employer offers some kind of match. You never want to leave any money on the table.

Make regular contributions into your Roth IRA until you reach the maximum allowed for the year (in 2013 it is $5,500, or $6,500 if you are fifty or older). Once you reach that limit, if there is still time to go in the year and you can swing depositing more into your retirement accounts, immediately notify your 401(k) plan administrator that you wish to increase your contribution through the end of the year or until you reach the limit—yours or the one imposed by the IRS. Do this every year until you turn seventy and a half (the age at which you must begin to take distributions from retirement accounts), and you will rack up a good-sized nest egg, some of which you will enjoy tax-free in retirement.

As flawed as I believe an employer's payroll deduction retirement savings plan may be, given its high fees and the ability of the government to change the rules of the game, you need to join. Even with its faults, it is still a good thing. If you do not participate, chances that you will save on your own with the same regularity and intensity are slim to none. Even if fees are too high in some plans—that can be particularly true in small-company plans administered by insurance companies—the tax and match benefits typically offset the costs. Even then you should push your employer to look for less expensive options.

Call your human resources department first thing tomorrow morning and ask to meet with a counselor. Find out the terms and conditions of your company's plan. Listen carefully for how much they match. Ask questions, and keep asking until you understand how your plan works. You may be surprised to learn that your company automatically enrolls all employees, then gives them the option to opt out.

One Last Thing

Your retirement savings plans are not part of your Contingency Fund. Retirement is a long-term need, and your retirement funds should not be 100 percent liquid. Your retirement accounts will be invested in a variety of equities, bonds, and mutual funds. Trying to get your hands on that money will be very costly and somewhat difficult.

Your Contingency Fund is for short-term needs and should remain liquid at all times. Many people save only for retirement and have no liquid savings for emergencies. Confusion over this matter has been the reason why many Americans have found themselves having to borrow from their 401(k) and other long-term savings to cover short-term needs.

You can avoid this trap by making sure you have your Contingency Fund in place for short-term emergencies before you begin to aggressively contribute funds to retirement plans and other types of investments.

9

Own Your Home Outright

Personally, the thought of being in a financial hole in old age gives me hives, and I'm working hard to make sure it doesn't happen.

Jennie L. Phipps

ome ownership in the United States has taken a beating in recent years. In fact, 79 percent of Americans say the Great Recession has caused the country to rethink the reasons for owning a home,[1] and high foreclosure rates have pushed the home ownership rate in the United States to a fifteen-year low.

But recent data suggest the housing market's outlook is promising. That's good news, because owning a home is an important part of retirement planning. And when I say "own," I mean you really own that piece of the earth free and clear of loans, mortgages, or liens before you retire or even sooner if at all possible. Here are the reasons:

1. A house is a hard asset because it is tangible and fungible (that means it can be sold or traded for some other hard asset of equal or greater value), and historically will appreciate in value.

2. A home is utilitarian, because while it remains a valuable asset, you can live in it and enjoy it. It is a place of safety, a refuge for you and your family where you can protect what is yours.

3. A paid-for home gives you the option of a rent-free, mortgage-free retirement. It's yours, and no landlord can give you notice to move out and no lender can file a foreclosure notice. It belongs to you. That is security you will cherish one day.

4. Not only will a paid-for home reduce your expenses in retirement, but it also will be a safety net or "solution of last resort." More about this later when we talk about reverse mortgages.

If you have a paid-for home, congratulations. If you are in the process of buying your home now, perhaps it's time to kick up your repayment plans so you can own it sooner rather than later. Last, for non–home owners, now is the time to get into the home ownership market. Values are down and so are interest rates. The sooner you can see your way clear to get started the better.

Here are some strategies to help you own a home faster than you dreamed possible.

Buy Half as Much as You Can Afford

I want to show you a strategy for buying a home and paying it off in record time so that you pay only a fraction of the interest you might otherwise have had to pay.

Here's our scenario. Jill, age thirty-two, is ready to buy her first home. She meets with a lender to get prequalified before she starts shopping. The news is good. She qualifies for a thirty-year, 80 percent loan up to $220,000 at a 4 percent fixed rate. In real numbers, this means the bank will lend her $220,000, provided she makes a $55,000 down payment, which she has saved in her credit union savings account. Jill is free to shop for a home priced at $275,000. Using a mortgage calculator, Jill discovers that under these terms her monthly mortgage payment will be $1,050. She's excited because she is currently paying $1,500 a month to rent a condo.

Should Jill buy a home under these terms and remain faithful to the monthly payments, thirty years from now she will make the final payment and own a home outright. In the process, she will repay the $220,000 she borrowed plus $158,113 in interest.

But Jill has another option. She can lower her expectations and opt to buy a home that is significantly below the amount she qualifies to borrow—a house that is about half the price. She qualifies for a $275,000 home, but in this scenario, she would look for one in the $137,500 range. Then she would choose to pay down this half-price home with full-price payments she knows she can afford, which would be $1,050 per month.

On a half-price home with a $137,500 sales price, Jill's down payment would be reduced to $27,500 and her mortgage would be $110,000 at 4 percent interest. Even though her loan documents would require lower monthly payments of $656, look what happens when she opts to make the higher $1,050 payments: Her thirty-year mortgage will be paid in full in only ten and a half years, and her total interest payment drops to $25,786.

But wait. There is one more thing Jill can do to make this even better. She can increase her down payment to the $55,000 she has saved, which is sitting in the bank, *and* make the higher payments. Look how this makes things get even more amazing: She will own the half-price home free and clear in 7.6 years, paying only $13,322 in interest.

Jill is young. At age thirty-two, she could have the half-price home paid off before she turns forty. Then she'd have plenty of options. One would be to sell the home at its increased market value of, say, $175,000 and do this all over again. Only this time, she'd likely qualify for a $500,000 home, but she could buy one for half the price at $250,000. Then by using the entire $175,000 for the down payment and making monthly payments equal to what she would have to make on the $500,000 home, she could pay off that mortgage in about eight years. It is not unreasonable to think that our friend Jill could quite easily own a home with a market value of $300,000 or more before she turns fifty—and do it with the money she would have had to pay for rent.

A Magical Way to Pay Off a Mortgage Fast

You may be familiar with something known generically as a biweekly (twice a month) mortgage payment plan. The theory is that by paying one-half of your mortgage payment every two weeks instead of one full payment once each month, in one year you will have made twenty-six half payments or the equivalent of thirteen monthly payments. (If you were to make semimonthly payments, you would make two payments per month or twenty-four half payments each year. That may sound like a trivial distinction, but that one extra monthly mortgage payment each year is the magic in this strategy.)

Using this tactic, it is possible to pay a thirty-year mortgage in about twenty-two years and avoid paying a lot of interest. The theory is great, but there are some important pitfalls to consider.

First, mortgage companies will not accept half payments unless you have enrolled in their biweekly mortgage payment program. And they charge fees for that—typically $400 or more to enroll and then an additional fee for each biweekly payment. Once enrolled, you're stuck with that plan too. Generally, you can't go back to monthly payments without a hassle, and of course, more fees.

There is a clever way you can make thirteen monthly payments each year on your own—without your mortgage company's permission or approval and while keeping your options open to go back to your regular payment schedule whenever you like.

Each month when you make your regular monthly mortgage payment, write a second check or make a second payment if you bank online equal to one-twelfth of one payment. Clearly write in the memo area "Principal Prepayment Only." If your regularly monthly payment is $1,200, you would write one check for $1,200 and a second check for $100 ($1,200 ÷ 12 = $100). Because this second check will arrive with your regular payment, it will be seen and credited as an overpayment, not a partial payment, unless your mortgage contains a prepayment penalty clause (rarely these days).

Repeat this each month. At the end of one year, you will have made the equivalent of thirteen monthly payments because your twelve $100 payments will add up to that thirteenth payment. Bingo! You have paid exactly what you would have with a biweekly plan without the fees and obligation to continue. If things get tight, you can always stop sending that extra check each month then start again as you are able.

One note of caution: Your mortgage is the last debt you want to pay off because it is a low-interest obligation that gives you a modicum of tax relief. If you are carrying credit card debt, student loan debt, or other high-interest, unsecured debt, you need to pay off this debt in full before you make additional mortgage payments.

When You Move, Take Your Equity with You

Paying off a home mortgage so that you own a home does not mean you have to stay in the same house until you make that final payment in fifteen or thirty years. You can move your equity from one home to the next without losing your momentum. But you must be committed to a plan to do this. Let me show you how.

By way of review, "equity" is the difference between your home's market value and the amount you owe on your mortgage. If you could realistically sell your home today for $250,000 and the current balance you owe on your mortgage is $184,000, the difference of $66,000 is your equity. As your mortgage is paid down and as your home appreciates in value, your equity increases proportionately.

The key to owning a home free and clear is to fiercely protect your equity. You must never think of your home as a kind of ATM that allows you to tap into the equity with a home equity loan or line of credit. You must not take cash out should you refinance your current mortgage to get a lower interest rate. If you do these things along the way, full ownership will elude you because you will always be resetting the clock on a new thirty-year mortgage or simply allowing your precious equity to leak out through some kind of equity loan.

To explain how to move your equity from one home to another, let's use a military family we'll call the Millers. To make this easy to understand, I'm going to use round numbers and simple terms.

The Millers buy their first home for $200,000 with a 10 percent down payment of $20,000 and a $180,000 mortgage. After two years of faithful payments, they get orders to relocate. They sell the house for $210,000. Over the two years, they've paid the mortgage down a bit, and now they owe $178,000. They come out of the sale with $32,000, which is their equity in cash ($210,000 − $178,000 = $32,000). Normally, they might see this as a windfall, money to buy a few things, take the kids to Disney World. But no, their equity is a precious asset, and they fiercely protect every nickel of it.

At their next assignment, homes are less expensive, and the Millers find a great one for $195,000. Now, even though they could get in with 10 percent down, they should not even consider it. To get on track to own a home free and clear one day, they need to pour that entire $32,000 of equity from the last home into the new home.

They secure a new mortgage for $163,000 ($195,000 − $32,000 = $163,000). The payments are lower than they've been used to making because their mortgage is smaller and they're paying a lower interest rate. However—pay attention because this is important—they opt to continue making the same larger payment they were making on the previous mortgage. This reduces their mortgage balance faster, which means their equity is also growing faster.

Two years go by and they have to move again. They sell this home for $199,000. The nice thing is that because of their increased payments each month, the mortgage has dropped to $155,000. They pack up their things and their $44,000 of equity and head for their next post.

Provided the Millers follow this kind of strategy—putting the entire amount of equity into the next home in the form of a down payment and buying in the same price range while making the larger monthly payments they've become accustomed to—they will easily own a home in full before they retire. And if that final home is not located where they wish to retire, they can sell it and buy another home in a location of their choice with cash.

It is important to point out that each transaction (selling one home and buying another) is going to incur closing costs and real estate commissions. This is unavoidable and will slow the process, as those items will nibble away at the equity. Still, this tactic will surely work for you provided you are doggedly determined not to spend a dime of your equity and always move it to the next property.

Deductibility

Plenty of reputable financial professionals would take issue with me in this matter of paying off a home mortgage—that such a move is not good for one's financial situation. Some would even advise an older person who owns her home outright to take out a new mortgage in order to deduct the interest on her federal tax return. Assuming that senior woman has income sufficient to require that she pay taxes, I do not find that to be a good reason for her to go into debt with a home mortgage, even though the interest would be deductible.

Here's how this would play out. She follows the advisor's advice and mortgages her home. She makes payments each month and at the end of the year can deduct $1,000, which is the mortgage interest she paid. She is in the 15 percent federal tax bracket. This means that by deducting $1,000 from her taxable income, the taxes she owes are reduced by $150 ($1,000 x 0.15 = $150). That means she has to pay $1,000 to get back $150. Who in her right mind would chose to have a mortgage to do that? In the absence of some kind of estate planning of which I am not aware, I would say that's just wrong thinking.

For me, getting a deduction for my mortgage interest is like a consolation prize. Until I can pay off my mortgage in full (may it be soon), the deduction eases the pain of having to pay interest. The truth is I don't want the deduction. I cannot wait until I don't have to pay any interest at all and can claim absolutely no mortgage interest on my federal and state tax returns.

Does that make sense to you? Would you choose to pay $1,000 so you can get $150 back? If it does make sense to you, I'll make you a better deal than the IRS. Send me $1,000 every year, and I promise to send back not $150 but $500! Guaranteed. I'll be watching my mail.

A Reverse Mortgage

If you watch TV, you know the term *reverse mortgage*, if for no other reason than it's nearly impossible to escape the cadre of aging male actors who've found a second career as pitchmen. Following a compelling message filled with promises that every retiree can get all kinds of free money, viewers are urged to call for a free DVD that will explain the magic of a reverse mortgage.

The promise is that cash-strapped seniors can stay in their own homes and receive tax-free cash without having to make monthly payments. Generally, that's true. But it's not quite as foolproof as the handsome pitchmen make it sound. While reverse mortgage programs do offer what they advertise, what the salespeople don't mention is what you need to know.

A reverse mortgage is a home equity loan for someone who is at least sixty-two that may allow that qualifying senior to stay in her home rent-free while using some of the money that purchased that home in the first place. A reverse mortgage does not have to be repaid until the borrower dies or leaves the property.

Generally, here is the way a reverse mortgage works in real life. Let's say your aunt Millie, a widow, owns her home outright, and it has a market value of $215,000. She's in great health but struggles to get by each month on her Social Security benefit check of $1,700, plus $500, which she receives from late Uncle Ned's pension.

Aunt Millie is cash poor. She has no savings to speak of and barely squeaks by every month paying her utilities, property taxes, food, gasoline, and health care co-pays. She doesn't have enough money to maintain or repair her home, to buy things she wants, or to travel to see her grandchildren. She needs to replace her car, but for now that's out of the question. It's frustrating because she is sitting on close to a quarter of a million dollars of home equity, which is completely out of her reach.

Millie can't get a traditional home equity loan or line of credit because she doesn't have a job and couldn't handle the monthly payments even if she could qualify. Aunt Millie, in theory, is a good candidate for a reverse mortgage. This type of mortgage would allow her to access some of her home's equity without the requirement to make monthly payments or ever repay the debt.

The lender would appraise her home and then agree to lend from 30 to 80 percent of its market value either in one lump sum or by check every month, depending on her age, the value of the home, current interest rates, and loan fees. Aunt Millie can continue to live in the home rent-free with no payments on the reverse mortgage, provided she lives up to the terms and conditions of the loan.

But don't get too excited for good ol' Aunt Mil quite yet. The loan doesn't simply disappear. It becomes a lien on the property just like any kind of mortgage or equity loan. It must be repaid when she moves out of the house or dies. At that point, the house is sold to pay off the reverse mortgage, including all compounded interest and fees.

Aunt Millie can stay in the property indefinitely even if she lives to be 110. The lender cannot charge her rent or force her to make payments on the debt. Once Aunt Millie moves, the lender or heirs will sell the home to satisfy the debt. If the house sells for more than the total amount required to repay the debt, including interest and fees, what's left goes to Aunt Millie's estate and heirs. If, on the other hand, the house has lost value or Aunt Millie lives so long that the full amount due exceeds the amount the house sells for, the lender can't come after any of Aunt Millie's other assets in her estate.

Conditions

A reverse mortgage is not all fun and games in which the borrower walks away with a big fat check. There are conditions and rules you need to know about should you or someone you care about consider a reverse mortgage.

- A borrower must be at least sixty-two years old.

- A borrower must own the property free and clear or have a very small mortgage that can be paid in full with proceeds of the reverse mortgage.

- The reverse mortgage can be the only lien or loan on the property.

- A borrower must occupy the property continuously as her permanent residence. If a borrower moves out for a period longer than twelve months, the loan becomes due, and the house must be sold to pay off the reverse mortgage.

- A borrower must keep the property in good repair and well maintained at her expense and to the lender's approval.

- A borrower must pay property taxes as they come due.

- A borrower must pay for home owners' insurance on the property in an amount required by the lender.

- A borrower must pay for mortgage insurance and keep the premiums current to protect the lender in the event that anything goes wrong—such as the property loses value or the borrower lives so long that there's not enough money in the deal to repay the lender.

- A borrower must attend free third-party counseling from a HUD-approved counselor before the reverse mortgage is funded.

Pros

Play and stay. You can tap into your home's equity and remain in the home for as long as you like. You do not have to make monthly payments or repay the debt until you leave the property.

Flexibility. Because you can take out equity as a lump sum, fixed monthly payments, or line of credit (or any combination thereof), a reverse mortgage offers a great deal of flexibility.

Capped value. The total amount owed can never exceed the current value of the home, even if that value plummets. When the home is sold, after paying off the reverse mortgage plus interest and fees, the remaining proceeds go to you or your estate.

Cons

There are many things to consider before pulling the trigger on a reverse mortgage. Here are a few.

Expensive. Reverse mortgages are subject to huge fees and expenses, which are paid to the lender upfront out of the home's equity.

Compounding interest. Even though no monthly payments are required, a reverse mortgage accrues interest each month. Since you aren't paying it, that interest due gets tacked onto the outstanding principal balance. Next month, interest accrues on that larger balance, meaning you'll be paying interest on interest. And away it grows! This is known as "compounding," which I believe is Latin for "reproducing like rabbits."

Must stay. Once you have a reverse mortgage, you and/or your spouse have to live in the property or repay the loan in its entirety. You do have a twelve-month grace period, but that could be wiped out by an extended illness or surgery that involves convalescing in a care facility. Stay away for twelve months and one day and the loan must be repaid, even if that means you must sell the house.

Effects eligibility. The proceeds from a reverse loan could prove a barrier to qualifying for Medicaid, where having a lot of equity in a home might not.

Tapping in too early. Reverse mortgages, first introduced in the 1960s, were designed to come to the rescue of cash-strapped seniors in their late seventies and eighties who were facing the high cost of paying for nursing home care for one spouse while the other spouse remained at home. These days, more and more baby boomers are looking to these loans to shore up their financial resources so they can stop working, pay off their credit cards, travel, and enjoy life.

Think of a reverse mortgage not as an added benefit to owning a home but as a tool of last resort to be considered many years from now, and only when every other resource or option has been exhausted. Then if you must use it, you will be grateful to have it and to have planned well.

10

Build Your Personal Investment Portfolio

Retirement investing is not about saving for next year. It's about saving for the long term—indeed, the very long term. In some cases that's 20, 30, or even 50 years out.

James O'Donnell

As awesome as your Contingency Fund is and as important as your 401(k) and Roth IRA are, at their very best, those strategies are not enough to grow the money you are going to need in retirement.

Your Contingency Fund is not an investment. It is not positioned for growth. It is an emergency fund being kept safe in a savings account.

Your 401(k) and Roth IRA, because of the tax advantages allowed by the government, are seriously restricted. The government tells you how much you can deposit into those accounts each year. Never allow yourself to assume that if you have maxed out your 401(k) and Roth IRA each year that your retirement income is set, that you've arrived.

A personal investment portfolio is the way to boost the resources you will need in retirement. And this raises a problem. Many women do not feel comfortable with the idea of investing. The word *investing* sends shivers of fear up and down their spines and turns their palms sweaty.

Many people believe that only highly trained investment professionals with professional certifications such as Certified Financial Planner or My Son the Stockbroker are capable of understanding the complexities of investing. But that is not true. You are more than capable of creating, funding, and maintaining a respectable personal investment portfolio. You are! And that is exactly what I am going to suggest you do.

Trust me. An actively managed, stressfully watched, and overly expensive personal investment portfolio is not at all what I'm talking about. The best way I can describe a passive portfolio is to liken it to a slow cooker.

I love to cook, but I don't have the time or the gourmet abilities to make that the top priority of my life. That's why I have a slow cooker. It makes my life so much easier by appealing to my desire not to spend a small fortune eating out or hours making a from-scratch meal. In fact, the actual time it takes me to put together a fabulous meal is a fraction of what it would take to find a parking place, wait to be seated, read the menu, place an order, and finally get a meal on the table at a restaurant. And there's just nothing like anticipating walking through the door after a long day and getting that first whiff of simmering pot roast, slow cooker lasagna, or any number of other amazing dishes that come from this simple yet amazing kitchen appliance.

Not only are slow-cooked meals economical, but they are also forgiving. It doesn't matter if things are measured precisely or mixed perfectly or if I leave the six-hour chicken supreme cooking for eight. It never disappoints. And talk about trouble-free. It takes five minutes in the morning to dump five ingredients into the cooker to ensure that pot roast will be our fare that evening.

Wouldn't it be great if we could do the same with investing? Toss a few bucks into an account somewhere, set the parameters, and forget about it. Then some time in the future look in the account and be pleasantly surprised by how it all turned out. That's exactly the kind of a passive personal investment portfolio I want to introduce to you. It's a plan that is simple, automatic, and self-managing. I'm going to show you how you can set it and forget it.

You will not need the services of an investment professional (stockbroker, financial planner). Despite investment professionals wanting you to believe that investing is difficult, something that should not be handled by amateurs like us, you do not need a professional, nor do you need an advanced degree in finance to make your own investment decisions. But before we get into the details of a simple portfolio, let's go over the basics of investing.

The Basics of Investing

Investing is the act of exposing money to risk with the expectation of receiving a reward or "return" of more money. There is a direct correlation between risk and return. The greater the risk, the greater the potential return. Less risk, less return.

Investing is not speculation. Speculation requires levels of risk that personal investors should not even consider taking.

Speculators are looking for huge returns in brief periods of time. Anyone who promises that you can double your money in a matter of months is not offering you an investment but asking you to speculate.

Investing is not gambling. Gambling involves games of chance and wagering opportunities. Unlike with investing, the chances of losing when gambling far exceed those of winning.

Investing is an activity that we as stewards of God's resources are unavoidably called to do (Matt. 25:14–30).

There are only two ways you can invest your money—either as an owner or as a lender. When you buy stock in a company, you become a part owner or "shareholder" of the company. Most major companies that are publicly traded have millions of shares divided up among many people and financial institutions, all of which are owners of that company. If the company prospers and creates greater profits, the stock becomes more valuable, which increases its value and pushes its price higher. An investor's goal is to buy low and sell high in order to realize a profit or "gain" on her investment.

When you invest in bonds, you are lending money to an individual, a company, the US Treasury, or a local government entity. Bonds are created when an organization (called the issuer) decides that it wants to borrow a certain sum of money from investors. As with any other loan, the issuer promises to pay the money back plus interest. You will hear this rate of interest called the "coupon rate." At the end of the term, a bond matures and the issuer repays the lender the original amount borrowed plus interest.

Sounds easy, doesn't it? Pick some winning stocks, sit back while the price goes up, then sell and pocket your profits. Or buy some bonds that are paying high rates of interest, wait for them to mature, then collect your original investment plus the interest. Getting rich never sounded so easy!

But it's not that easy. What's the problem?

Even if you were some kind of a whiz kid with an uncanny ability to pick winning stocks every time, you'd need to devote full time to the endeavor. You could hire a professional to forecast the future and pick winning stocks for you. The problem with that is nobody knows for sure what's coming next year, next month, next week, or even tomorrow. Nobody. Market forecasts are not only confusing but also conflicting, misleading, and potentially costly to those who make their investment decisions based on them.

Another problem is that every time you pick a winner and then sell a loser, you pay a hefty sales commission. Even the discount brokerage firms' commissions add up quickly and can blow through profits like a crazed shopper ripping through a credit limit at a Nordstrom semiannual sale!

I can tell you from experience and years of observation and research that this type of investing is not easy. Every time you buy or sell a stock (or bond), there is somebody somewhere on the other end of the transaction buying what you're selling or selling what you're buying. More than likely it's an MBA-toting Wall Street stockbroker or the manager of a pension or mutual fund. What they have that you don't is access to expensive research and portfolio management software. It's a competitive game, and you have as much chance of consistently beating those folks as you have of winning the Pillsbury Million Dollar Bake-Off on your first try.

Not quite ready for that? No problem. There's a better way.

Enter mutual funds. A mutual fund pools money together from thousands of small investors, and then its professional investor or "fund manager" buys stocks, bonds, or other securities with the money. The advantage is that a small inves-tor can diversify by owning lots of different stocks and have them "actively managed" professionally. The fund manager's job is to search for great stocks to make that fund return profits that beat the market, which means a return on your investment that is better than the market index you've chosen to compare to (S&P 500, Dow, etc.). Let's say that last year the Dow increased 10 percent. Every mutual fund manager and individual investor, for that matter, hopes he or she was able to return a gain that exceeded 10 percent, which in this case would be considered the Dow Jones Industrial Average's annual return.

Mutual funds hold a lot of promise because not only do you own the shares but you also get the full-time services of a professional team who looks after your shares by making appropriate buys and sells in order to improve gains and increase the amount by which the fund beats the market.

All of that "active management" does not come cheaply. Not only do mutual funds charge a "load" or fee to buy in (some funds push this fee to the back end and collect it when you sell), but they also charge hefty maintenance fees. Re-search costs and high-end salaries for the fund manager and support staff can significantly run up operating costs, which the fund must charge the shareholders. In fact, some funds' "expense ratio," which is what the fund charges investors an-nually for the costs of running the fund, can come in as high as 3 percent, calculated as a percentage of the amount you have invested. These days when a 2 percent gain is considered adequate, that kind of fee can turn a marginal winner into a big loser!

You may already be asking yourself, *Why work so hard to beat the market, then turn around and have to pay out big fees that effectively eat up all of those gains?* Bingo. You're very smart to have noticed this seeming conflict.

Before I respond to that, let me introduce a particular type of mutual fund known as an "index fund." To understand, you first need to know about indexes. The Dow, the S&P 500, the Nasdaq 100, and the Wilshire 5000 are all lists or "indexes." There are others, but these are the most well known. Each is a group of stocks on a list chosen to represent portions of the stock market.

An index fund is a type of mutual fund whose assets are the exact stocks on a given list or index. For example, the S&P 500 is an index that tracks the performance of 500 of the largest companies in America. An index fund based on the S&P 500 would simply purchase shares in all five hundred of those companies—no buying, selling, or high-priced analysts required. If the S&P 500 were to gain 12 percent in one year, the index fund's gain would match that because the fund holds the same stocks.

Index funds have very low fees because they don't need fund managers. There's no need to invest in an index fund with an expense ratio greater than 0.40 percent (that's four-tenths of one percent). And there's no need for analysis or research. Index funds are what they are, and they are designed to match—not beat—the index they track.

Let me say this again. The goal of "actively managed" mutual funds is to beat the market. The goal of "passively managed" index funds is to match the particular segment of the market they track.

There are untold numbers of index funds. There are those that track the performance of the entire US stock market, while others track certain sectors of the market such as health care, the pharmaceutical industry, international stock markets, the bond market of any country, and just about anything else you can imagine.

Back to your question, "Why work so hard to beat the market, then turn around and have to pay out big fees that effectively eat up all of those gains? Wouldn't investors be better off just buying index funds?"

Interestingly, research confirms that most investors actually would be better off in index funds.[1] Passively managed index funds beat actively managed mutual funds year after year. It's almost uncanny but seems to point to the fact that humans—and I'm speaking specifically of fund managers now—are not infallible. All their research, charting, and predictions cannot consistently beat the market.[2] And due to the high costs of active management, the majority of actively managed mutual funds fail to outperform their respective indexes. Actively managed funds might beat the market from time to time, but by the time the shareholders pay all the fees it costs to pull that off, they're worse off than if they'd simply put their money into index funds.[3]

This is not to say that all mutual funds fail to beat the market. Some hot funds do now and then. But none is consistent year after year. It is difficult, if not impossible, to predict ahead of time which actively managed funds will be the top performers.

Let me be really clear about this: Index funds are not automatic winners year after year. If an index such as the S&P 500 has a bad year, the index fund that tracks its performance will suffer the same outcome. You have no control over that. And while past performance does not guarantee future outcomes, common sense tells us that being the owner of a profitable company is a financially good thing. That's precisely what you're doing when you invest in broadly diversified stock index funds. You're investing in companies so that you can receive a share of their profits.

Is every company profitable? Of course not. However, if you own a portion of each of the publicly traded companies in the United States (as well as a few thousand companies in other countries), you can be confident that, on the whole, those companies will earn a net profit. Over time, that profit will be returned to the shareholders in the form of dividend payments and increases in net asset value (NAV) of the shares.

Building a lifetime investment portfolio on a well-diversified group of index funds will give you the best shot at making a reasonable return over the years while requiring the least amount of your attention.

An Index Fund Portfolio

Are you beginning to think pot roast? You should, because here's where an index fund portfolio takes on the characteristics of a slow cooker. An ideal start would look like this.

1. You open an account at one of the companies I recommend below and make an initial purchase into three index funds. (You can create a user name and password on the company's website, but please take the time to call and speak with an advisor to actually set up and fund your investment account.)

2. At the same time, set up an automatic purchase plan wherein you are adding more shares each month to your account. This is important, even if you start with an initial amount of only $50 a month. For most investors, investing what's left over after covering expenses each month doesn't work. That's because nothing is ever left over! When you automate your investing, you change things around so that you invest first, then spend what's left over.

The single most important thing you can do to have enough money in reserve to retire someday is to save and invest regularly, year in and year out, over a period of multiple decades. If you do not automate, between procrastination and forgetfulness, it's extremely unlikely that you will take the time to write and mail a check to your brokerage firm every month for thirty years.

3. Forget it. Just like the chicken taco soup we're having for dinner tonight. Don't peek obsessively. You do know that for each time you lift the lid on your slow cooker you need to add another twenty-five minutes to the cook time, right? Same with your portfolio. Each time you peek or hover obsessively over a momentary market downturn, you open the door to making an impulsive decision to cash in or make a trade that could result in unintended consequences, such as creating a taxable event. If you just leave it be and let it grow, your index fund portfolio will bring you great comfort and satisfaction one day when the time is right for you to retire.

When the market is down, your automatic purchase plan will net more shares into your account. When the market is up, you'll be purchasing fewer shares, but your NAV will be up. Just keep buying every month come rain or shine.

Over the years, you may want to add funds into your portfolio and make other kinds of rebalancing moves. But generally speaking, this initial setup should last you for many years. Just keep investing and adding every month.

Three Basic Portfolios

When selecting a brokerage company for constructing an index fund portfolio, these should be your three primary considerations.

Expense ratio. This is the annual management fee charged to each shareholder of a mutual fund (remember, an index fund is simply a type of mutual fund), expressed as a percentage. The expense ratio is the most reliable indicator of that fund's future performance. Actively managed mutual funds can have expense ratios as high as 4 percent, while index funds are well under one-half of 1 percent, and many are much lower than that. As a rule of thumb, never choose an index fund with an expense ratio greater than 0.40 percent. When choosing between two similar index funds for your portfolio, choose the one with the lowest expense ratio.

Minimum investment per fund. This is the smallest dollar amount you must have to fund a new account in your portfolio. Note that companies often waive the minimum requirement when you sign up to have a certain amount withdrawn automatically from your checking account each month and deposited into your account to buy more shares. Just tell the customer service person you speak with how much you want to invest each month and which funds you want in your portfolio to start, and you'll be all set.

Selection of funds. You want to place your index fund investment portfolio with a company that offers a good selection of index funds. Looking to the future, you want a company with enough funds for you to build a diversified portfolio. This assumes that in time you will add more index funds to your portfolio.

What follows are examples of three low-cost index funds portfolios with Vanguard, Fidelity, and Schwab, all of which fit the criteria outlined above. I am not suggesting that these are the only companies offering index funds. These examples represent the kind of well-rounded approach to diversifying your personal investing portfolio. Each suggested portfolio has a total market fund, an international fund, and a bond fund, which appropriately spreads your risks and makes sure that all of your eggs are not in one basket.

Vanguard Index Funds[4] (Vanguard.com; 800-252-9578)

1. Vanguard Total Stock Market Index Fund (expense ratio: 0.18 percent)
2. Vanguard Total International Stock Index Fund (expense ratio: 0.22 percent)
3. Vanguard Total Bond Market Index Fund (expense ratio: 0.22 percent)

   Minimum investment: $3,000 minimum initial investment per fund

Just for fun, let's jump into a time machine and go back a decade or so to 2002. You were smart enough to invest $10,000 in Vanguard's Total Stock Market Index Fund. Your money more than doubled to $21,255, or 8.45 percent growth before taxes. If you looked at a chart of this fund on Vanguard's website, which you can at http://bit.ly/cdUnQE, you would see how the economic crisis of 2008 affected this investment (there's a reason that it's called risk) but also how this fund recovered in the years that followed.

Fidelity Index Funds[5] (Fidelity.com; 800-343-3548)

1. Spartan Total Market Index Fund (expense ratio: 0.10 percent)
2. Spartan International Index Fund (expense ratio: 0.20 percent)
3. Spartan US Bond Index Fund (expense ratio: 0.22 percent)

Minimum investment: $2,500 minimum initial investment per fund

Schwab Index Funds[6] (Schwab.com; 866-232-9890)

1. Schwab Total Stock Market Index Fund (expense ratio: 0.09 percent)
2. Schwab International Index Fund (expense ratio: 0.19 percent)
3. Dreyfus Bond Market Index Fund (expense ratio: 0.40 percent)

Minimum investment: $100 minimum initial investment per fund

At the time of this writing, Schwab did not offer even one bond index fund. That said, an investor at Schwab would still have access to bond funds run by other companies, such as the Dreyfus Bond Market Index Fund mentioned above. Unless you are totally in love with the Schwab company, opening your account with Vanguard or Fidelity would keep things appropriately simple.

All three of these sample portfolios are set up so that you have one-third of your investment in domestic stocks, one-third in international stocks, and the last third in bonds. That is referred to as your asset allocation. Over time, this may get out of whack a bit if, for example, international stocks do very well one year while your bond fund lags. From time to time, you should take a look at your allocation and reconfigure it so that you are back to your intended allocation. You may wish to sell some of one fund to buy more in one of the others to create balance, or you might decide to change the way you allocate your monthly purchase to get back into balance.

Do not let balancing your portfolio cause you stress and worry, however. Taking a look once a year should be more than sufficient. When you see that your portfolio has strayed far from the allocation you desire, then you can take steps to rebalance it.

11

How Much Will I Need to Retire?

Question: "How much money is enough money?"
Answer: "Just a little more."

Reporter to John D. Rockefeller

How much money will you need to retire? That's the million-dollar question, isn't it? Every advisor and every website will give you a different and sometimes scary number. It may surprise you that my answer to this question is going to fly in the face of an entire financial planning industry. I don't know, you don't know, and no one else knows either.

It is impossible to know how much money you will need years from now when you retire. To give you a hard-and-fast answer presumes a level of certainty about the future that cannot be known. Let me show you why this is true.

To determine what some refer to as "the magic number," we need specific information:

How long will you live?

How much will you need each year to pay all of your bills and enjoy a comfortable retirement?

What is a "comfortable retirement"?

What will be your health status for the rest of your life?

How will the economy, taxes, and inflation behave during your retirement?

But just because we can't arrive at a specific number doesn't mean we shouldn't look at various ideas so we'll be better informed and prepared. You wouldn't leave for a long road trip without checking the gas gauge in your car, would you? If you break down the different approaches to this question, you'll find they fall into four basic categories.

The Educated Guess Approach

None of us knows how long we will live. Our days are known only to God. We can estimate based on certain genetic and lifestyle factors using online longevity calculators,[1] but the results remain educated guesses. These kinds of estimates do not take into account things such as disasters and accidents because they can't.

Statistically, the life expectancy of a woman in the northern hemisphere is currently 80.1. However, if she makes it to age 65, then her life expectancy increases to 85. A professional financial planner determining your financial needs in retirement would most likely go with 80.1 until you reach age 65, then adjust your needs upward to accommodate your longer life. Still, it's only a guess.

To get an idea of what your future living expenses will be, we need to know two things: (1) your current annual expenses and (2) an estimate of how these expenses will change.

If you track your expenses and spending pretty closely, you can look at the last twelve-month period to come up with the annual figure. If you are not a tracker already, you will need things such as credit card statements, bank statements, and payroll stubs, since some of your expenses may be deducted directly from your wages.

Once you have the annual figure, start making adjustments. For example, if you have a mortgage payment now, will that go away before you retire? You can deduct the amount you are currently saving for retirement. Take off a reasonable amount for work-related expenses such as transportation, union dues, dry cleaning, and so forth. Your health insurance premiums will change as you move from traditional coverage to Medicare with appropriate supplements. If you plan to travel or take up activities you've been postponing until you no longer work, come up with costs for these things and add them into your calculations.

You will need to adjust for inflation. Inflation measures the gradual increase in the cost of goods and services. Inflation accounts for the fact that gasoline cost twenty-five cents a gallon when I was a kid, and now it is nearly four dollars a gallon. It takes more money to buy gas, not because gas and oil have become more valuable but because our money has become less valuable, therefore taking more of it to buy things. Historically, inflation in the United States has averaged around 3 percent per year. We cannot predict the future, but we can use this figure to come up with a rough estimate.

Adjusting for taxes is necessary when estimating how much you'll need each year, but it is not an easy thing to do. If you move into a lower tax bracket, you'll pay less in taxes. However, if taxes increase, which many predict they will, you could be paying more in retirement than you are paying now even if you are in a lower bracket.

When determining whether you've saved enough to retire, the goal isn't to determine how much income you need each year but rather how much income you need each year from your savings and investments. To arrive at that figure, subtract any other income you expect to receive—Social Security benefits, pension income, a part-time job, etc.

In years past, the Social Security Administration sent you a statement right before your birthday providing an estimate of the Social Security benefits you could receive as a result of your earnings to date. The SSA now mails statements only to workers one time at age twenty-five and then again annually once workers reach age sixty and are not already receiving Social Security benefits.

Everyone else can check their Social Security statements online. Go to Social Security's MyStatement (ssa.gov/my statement/) and create a "My Social Security" account. For security, you'll need to provide information about yourself that matches the information on file with the Social Security Administration, as well as some information that matches your Experian credit report. You will be able to check your current estimated benefits as well as your earnings record up to the point that the SSA has updated your account, which seems to lag by a year or two. It's a good idea to check statements for errors once a year.

If you expect to need $40,000 of pretax income each year, and you expect to receive a total of $20,000 from Social

Security and pension income, you need to fund $20,000 each year with your savings. Further, if you expect to live twenty years in retirement, you need at least twenty times $20,000, or $400,000, in retirement savings *plus* an adjustment for inflation and possibly taxes, depending on how tax rates and tax brackets change in the future. Keep in mind that these seriously rough figures do not allow for inflation or make any attempt to figure out what taxes will look like years or decades from now.

The Rules of Thumb Approach

Another approach is to pick one of the many rules of thumb from the financial planning industry. Here are several for your consideration.

In 2012, Fidelity Investments released new savings guidelines for retirement savings. According to Fidelity's calculation, most employees should aim to save at least eight times their ending salary in order to meet basic income needs in retirement.[2] This means that if you are earning $75,000 a year at the time you retire at age sixty-seven, you will need to have eight times $75,000, or $600,000, in retirement savings. To stay on track with that sum, savers should have about a year's pay put away by age thirty-five, three years' pay saved by forty-five, and five years' pay saved by fifty-five.

Another rule of thumb offered by State Farm Insurance is that you will need about 70 or 80 percent of your preretirement income in retirement.[3] Or 90 or 100 percent, reports *Money* magazine.[4] What this means is that if you make $50,000 annually prior to retirement, you should plan on needing between $35,000 and $50,000 for each year you plan to live in retirement. It all depends on the experts you listen to.

A 2008 study by Hewitt Associates, provider of human capital and management consulting services since the 1940s, concluded that due to rising health care costs, retirees will spend a whopping 126 percent of their preretirement income each year in retirement.[5]

The Rough Estimate Approach

Mike Piper, CPA and founder of the popular Oblivious Investor blog, ObliviousInvestor.com, offers a reasonable and quite useful approach for answering the question of how much you will need in retirement savings. You can do it in just three steps:

1. Determine your annual retirement spending needs in today's dollars that will be funded by your retirement savings.
2. Adjust upward for inflation.
3. Multiply by twenty-five.

Take a deep breath. I'm going to show you a mathematical formula that Piper offers to determine the amount you will need in retirement.

$$R = C \times (1 + I)^T$$

Here's an explanation for these terms:

R: Your annual retirement spending needs

C: Retirement spending in today's dollars

I: Projected annual rate of inflation

T: The number of years until you retire

You determine that you will need $40,000 per year during retirement. You are fifteen years away from retiring, and you expect inflation to average 3 percent per year over those two decades. Your calculation would be as follows[6]:

$$R = \$40,000 \times (1.03)^{15} = \$62,319$$

You will be eligible to receive Social Security benefits, and the estimate at the ssa.gov site is that you will receive $1,800 per month, or $21,600 per year.

$$\$62,319 - \$21,600 = \$40,719$$

This is the amount you will need to provide from your retirement savings each year in retirement. Finally, multiply by twenty-five to come up with the amount you will need to save before retirement.

$$\$40,719 \times 25 = \$1,017,975$$

The Focus on Expenses Approach

Another school of thought suggests that if you are going to estimate anything in preparation for retirement, you should estimate your expenses first and work backward from there. I find this approach to be much saner than attempting to predict what things are going to cost many years from now.

By reducing expenses now and ahead of retirement, you free up more money to save and invest. By going into retirement with no mortgage, no rent, no debts, and low monthly expenses, you can dramatically reduce the amount you will need to live on once you stop earning income.

Unless you make drastic lifestyle changes, you as a retiree are most likely to spend the same as, if not more than, you did before retirement. This approach to retirement planning suggests that you take your full expenses upon retirement and add 10 percent to that figure, which is a reasonable amount to cover increased costs (inflation) and rising taxes. But then you could turn around and deduct the 10 percent because you won't have the "expense" of saving aggressively for retirement while in retirement.

Taking this approach would certainly inspire me to come up with ways to cut back expenses. It would prompt me to consider moving to an area with an extremely low cost of living. I would also think about doing my world traveling while I have a steady income.

We can wrap up this discussion with this salient conclusion: Reducing your personal cost of living is the most reasonable way to approach retirement planning, whether you are close to it or far from it.

In Conclusion

Exhausting, isn't it? Predicting expenses, inflation, and taxes makes my head spin. I think that may be why Jesus told his disciples:

> Therefore I tell you, do not worry about your life, what you will eat or drink; or about your body, what you will wear. Is not life more than food, and the body more than clothes? Look at the birds of the air; they do not sow or reap or store away in barns, and yet your heavenly Father feeds them. Are you not much more valuable than they? Can any one of you by worrying add a single hour to your life? And why do you worry about clothes? See how the flowers of the field grow. They do not labor or spin. Yet I tell you that not even Solomon in all his splendor was dressed like one of these. (Matt. 6:25–29)

Notice, this doesn't say not to look to the future or plan for the future. A good money manager always puts aside money for the future while living in the present. Jesus said not to be anxious, not to obsess, and not to worry about the future. You may need more, not less, in retirement. Plan accordingly and start saving. If you are already saving, save more.

12

Can I Count on Social Security for My Retirement?

The fundamental question is not how much longer the Social Security and Medicare trust funds are going to be solvent. The question is how much we're willing to spend to insure that the elderly have affordable access to health care and some financial security.

James Surowiecki in the *New Yorker*

Since the day I got my Social Security number when I was still in high school, I've heard this tiny voice out there somewhere telling me that Social Security will not be around by the time I reach retirement age. I will be one of millions who contribute all of my working life and never see a dime in my old age. That voice became louder and louder through the years as I became more convinced I would be shut out. And I've done my share of affirming that prediction, quite

certain that I and my peers would come out with the short
stick on that deal.

Quite remarkably, that voice has quieted for me. In fact, I
may have to eat my words. I have received confirmation that
as this book goes to publication, my first check has been
approved for delivery.

Will the system endure so that one day you will have that
same assurance? I cannot answer that question with certainty.
But here is what we do know from the most recent Social
Security trustees' annual report[1]: The trustees now project
that the old age and disability trust funds combined will be
unable to pay full benefits in 2033, three years sooner than
projected in last year's report. Come 2033, if Congress does
nothing, there will be sufficient assets to pay 75 percent of
the benefits. In other words, while the money the country has
been collecting in imaginary trust funds will have run out by
2033, the taxes coming in should still be enough to pay $0.75
for every dollar of promised retirement benefits[2] beginning in
2033. To make the system work, Congress will have to reduce
benefits, increase taxes, or, more likely, do both.

At best, when these kinds of changes go into effect, they
could easily turn Social Security from a guaranteed annuity
for all into a safety net for the very poor. As it is now, even at
best—meaning that you do receive 100 percent of the benefits
for which you will be eligible when you reach full retirement
age—the benefits will not be enough. The average Social Security benefit for women sixty-five and older in 2012 was about
$12,700 per year[3]—slightly more than $1,000 per month.

Social Security is not an investment program. There is no
individual bank account out there with your name on it that
contains all of the money you have paid into the system since
you got your first job. The money you have contributed has

not been invested wisely to assure you financial independence when you retire. Social Security is insurance designed to insulate you from having to live under a bridge in your old age. It is meant to provide you with a steady check that you cannot outlive or lose in a stock market downturn.

No one will ever accuse the Social Security program of being too simple or not having enough rules and regulations. The Social Security website (ssa.gov) is surprisingly user-friendly, but it is so vast and cumbersome to search that I want to offer you a more reasonable resource. Most of what I know about Social Security I have learned from a small yet mighty book titled *Social Security Made Simple: Social Security Retirement Benefits and Related Planning Topics Explained in 100 Pages* by Mike Piper. I cannot recommend this book and all of Piper's "made simple" books enough. They are as represented: simple to read.

Between Piper's blog Oblivious Investor (ObliviousInvestor .com), his books, and his presence on the online forum Bogle heads.org, I have gained something equivalent to an undergraduate degree in matters of simple investing. Piper is an independent CPA, licensed in Missouri, who is a prolific writer with the ability to cut out all the noise and make complicated concepts, terms, and calculations easy to understand.

As for your question about whether you will be able to count on Social Security, we can assume with a reasonable level of certainty that it will still exist when you retire. The details, however, such as how much you will receive each month, at what age you can receive it, and what that benefit will translate into in terms of buying power at the time, cannot be predicted with any level of certainty.

13

The Value of Time

Time is your most precious gift because you only have a set amount of it. You can make more money, but you can't make more time.

Rick Warren

You may have noticed what seems like two opposing themes running throughout the previous chapters.

The first: Start saving early. Due to the miracle of compounding growth, the earlier you start, the less you'll have to contribute to end up with more than if you started late. The other important theme is aimed at those who cannot identify with the first: It's only too late if you don't start now. No matter where you are or how little you think you have, start now. Today. Start. Saving.

These principles are not in conflict. It's just that one is much easier than the other. The longer you wait to get started, the more difficult the task will be. That's because you may have to save twice as much in far less time, and even then you may not be able to make up for lost time.

No matter how and when you get started with saving for retirement, it is better than not starting at all. Having saved some is better than having saved nothing. The longer you delay, the more difficult it will be to get started.

Consider two savers, Ashley and Zoe. Ashley starts at age twenty and saves $2,000 a year for ten years and then stops saving altogether. With 7 percent growth, she would have $315,676 by age sixty-five.

Zoe saves nothing until age forty, then socks away twice as much each year—$4,000 for twenty-five years, more than twice as long as Ashley. Even with this aggressive catch-up plan, Zoe falls short of Ashley's total, socking away just $270,705 by age sixty-five.

Imagine now that Ashley did not stop saving after ten years but kept putting away $2,000 each year throughout her working life. She'd have $611,503 by age sixty-five. If she increased the contribution to $4,000 at age forty, to match Zoe's annual number, she'd have almost $750,000 at retirement. Ashley's advantage comes in the fact that every year as her investment grows, that growth also begins to grow. And she got that ten-year head start on Zoe.

This reminds me of Aesop's fable of the tortoise and the hare. The tortoise starts out slow and easy and just keeps up that pace. The hare, on the other hand, is erratic. He takes naps, sleeps too long, and tries to sprint to make up for lost time. The hare is easily distracted, hyperactive, and frequently takes his eyes off the goal. In the end, of course, the tortoise wins because, as the moral of the story goes, slow and steady wins the race.

Compounding interest is the secret in all of this. As interest or growth occurs, instead of withdrawing that gain from the account, you leave it in to increase your principal. Now your interest begins to earn interest, and it becomes exponential growth. Saving early is the nearly painless trick to building retirement security. It's the only true silver bullet.

I love this fictionalized story about Christopher Columbus because it illustrates rather dramatically the power of compounding interest.

In 1492, Christopher Columbus decided he was going to save for retirement. He had one penny ($0.01), and he knew he could earn 6 percent every year on his money. He put the penny in his left pocket and placed the interest ($0.01 x 6% = $0.0006) in his right pocket for safekeeping. He never added anything to his original penny in his left pocket. Yet the interest accumulated year after year in his right pocket.

Chris is a very healthy guy. He lives until today—521 years later—and decides to retire. So he takes his one penny from his left pocket and adds it to the simple interest in his right pocket. Want to guess how much Mr. Columbus has?

Well, the interest in his right pocket adds up to only $0.31 (521 years x $0.0006 = $0.3126). Along with his original penny from his left pocket, he has about $0.32 on which to retire. Not very good planning.

What could Chris have done differently? Let's assume Chris was much more astute about investing because he knew about compounding. Instead of putting the interest in his right pocket, he put it in his left pocket with the original penny— the principal. Over the years, he earned the same 6 percent interest on the original penny and the accumulated interest in his left pocket.

As the story goes, at the end of year one, he had $0.0106 in his left pocket (the original penny plus the 6 percent interest). At the end of year two, he had $0.011236 ($0.0106 plus the 6 percent interest). At the end of year three, he had $0.01191 ($0.011236 plus the 6 percent interest). This is called compounding and continued for Chris until today, 521 years later. How much has good ol' Chris finally accumulated for retirement?

The answer is somewhat more to Chris's liking. At the end of 521 years of compounding the original penny at 6 percent interest, Chris has $348,512,293,164.41 (that's 348 billion, 512 million, 293 thousand, 164 dollars, and 41 cents).[1] That's a lot of pocket change.

In its absurdity, this little story carries a powerful punch. You do not have to begin rich to benefit from compounding growth. You need to be disciplined and smart enough to start early.

14

Quick Guide to
Planning by Decades

Whoever gathers money little by little makes it grow.

Proverbs 13:11

You've likely heard more than a few times that hindsight is 20/20. It's true. Who among us cannot look in the rearview mirror of life and see things more clearly?

While I am determined not to live my life with regret, there are a few things I wish I'd known sooner. Like how the decisions I made in my twenties would throw my thirties into a major tailspin. Had I known, or cared, perhaps I could have avoided some very costly mistakes.

What follows are simple guidelines or benchmarks for each decade of life as it relates to preparing for retirement.

In Your Twenties

This is your defining decade and by far the most important decade for retirement planning. You're younger—and probably poorer—than you'll ever be again. And smart? Way smart given the fact that you're already thinking about retirement planning! Laying the groundwork now can make all the difference for you in the years to come.

What you're experiencing now in your twenties may not feel big enough or important enough to have anything close to a lifetime impact. Your income is low, your debts may be high, and you may feel as though you're living on the financial edge. Even though what you are experiencing now may not appear to be important, the truth is that big events of life don't always start out big.

I can certainly attest to the truth of this. Remember that mind-numbing amount of debt I ran up, the sum of which could have funded not only my retirement but that of my husband as well? I didn't start out with one big whopping purchase of $10,000 on a credit card. My debt started out small, totally inconsequential.

I counted heavily on the fact that I was young. Time was on my side. I assured myself that even if everything fell apart, I had plenty of time to start over. Was I ever wrong. I did not recognize what would become one of the most defining moments of my life during my twenties. My debt impacted my life severely and had long-lasting effects.

Listen, I know that dealing with the responsibility of your retirement may not be high on your list of priorities if you feel broke and overwhelmed by the stresses of getting started in life. Forty-five years from now seems like another lifetime. I get it. But perhaps you have your doubts that Social Security will be there for you. And you know that whatever it may look like, you don't want to rely on Social Security alone for a secure retirement.

The good news is that because you are young you haven't picked up a lot of bad financial habits. You have time to build a solid financial life. And the sooner you get on with that, the less it is going to cost you in the future to make up for any mistakes you make because you will make far fewer of them.

Develop your financial intelligence. Start by becoming an effective money manager (chaps. 4 and 5). Get your act together now by putting together a spending plan. That is the best way to take control of your finances. Assign every dollar that flows into your life a job to do, then follow up to make sure it did as it was told.

Start an emergency fund and get out of debt. Build your emergency fund as quickly as you can (chap. 6). This will give you the cushion you need to weather unexpected expenses and emergencies without having to raid your retirement savings. If you're in debt, fix that now and not later (chap. 7).

Open a retirement savings account. Join and participate in your employer's retirement savings plan, at least to the match, as soon as you qualify. Open and fund a Roth IRA as well. Consider yourself on track if you are regularly contributing 5 percent of your annual income to retirement savings. For example, if you are contributing 3 percent to get the match at work, make sure you are funding your Roth IRA with an additional 2 percent. And don't forget to adjust those deposits as you receive salary increases, even if the amounts feel so minuscule to be insignificant. That's the point! Start small and the impact is far less, well, impactful!

Stay physically, emotionally, and spiritually fit. Retirement preparation is not all about money. It also involves building and maintaining physical health by watching what you eat and exercising—both of which are much easier to begin when you're young and filled with energy. Investing in relationships will nurture your emotional health, while deepening your walk with God will keep you spiritually fit.

Your twenties matter. By making a decision now to start saving and preparing for the years you will spend in retirement—no matter how far away they seem—you will make a life-changing decision you will never regret.

In Your Thirties

Your college loans are probably paid off; you may be married and starting a family. You have career goals, but you haven't reached your full earning potential. If you want to retire by age sixty-seven, you have about thirty years. If you've been saving, you're on your way. But if you've put it off, it's time to catch up.

Fund your 401(k) and a Roth IRA. If your employer offers a 401(k), participate at least to the point of the match (if there is one) so you don't leave any free money on the table. Also open a Roth IRA and make funding it to the maximum each year a top priority. Set up automatic deposits to do this so you won't have to rely on your memory or make that "Will I or won't I?" decision every time you get a paycheck. Because you now have more financial responsibilities, you may be tempted to forgo saving for retirement, but don't do it. Time is still on your side, but the window is beginning to close.

Lots of things are going to compete for your savings and 401(k) contributions. Your career by now is on course, and perhaps you are ready to start a family or buy a house. You and your spouse are sure to experience lifestyle "creep" as you feel it's time to add things to your life. A new car or two, new furniture, and much-deserved vacations will challenge your determination to live an understated lifestyle. Your biggest challenge is to hold the reins on your spending.

Buy a home. Siphon off a down payment from the savings you have been growing with 10 percent of your take-home pay. Do not give into the temptation to buy the most expensive home you can afford. Instead, buy half the home you can afford, then make the largest payments you can afford (chap. 9). Your goal is to own this home outright as soon as possible. Do not enter into any home equity loans. That's a way to shoot yourself in the foot.

Don't succumb to consumer debt. Should you become a parent and home owner in the same decade, you could certainly build a case for taking on a lot of debt. Fight it. Don't give in by making sure you limit debt to a mortgage. And if you have run up debt, get out as quickly as you can. You'll be grateful in years to come if you hang tough now.

Set a goal for college savings. When the babies are born is the time to start saving for college. You may be squeezed already, but now is the time to determine your philosophy on who pays for college. You do not want to go into debt for this. If you plan to pay for all or part of your child's education, do that with money you have saved and invested, not with loans you take on in eighteen to twenty years. Run the scenarios at SavingforCollege.com. Here's an example. To meet 50 percent of the total cost of four years at a public university, based on the current average annual cost ($17,131) and a 6 percent inflation rate for college costs, you'd need to save $222 a month for eighteen years, assuming a 7 percent annual after-tax return on your college savings fund. To cover half of only the tuition bill, you'd need to save $107 a month.

As for which account to pump money into, your best bet is usually a state-sponsored 529 savings plan (find information on all of these state plans at SavingforCollege.com), which lets your savings accumulate tax-free. If you use the withdrawals for qualified educational expenses, such as tuition and fees, the earnings can be withdrawn tax-free as well. About two-thirds of the states also offer a tax benefit for contributing to a 529 plan.

Purchase life insurance. If there are people who depend on your income who would be in a desperate situation without it if you were to die, you need life insurance. If you are a stay-at-home mom without a formal paycheck, you too need life insurance that will cover the cost of all the jobs your husband would have to pay someone to do if he were to become a single parent. Here's some good news. Term life insurance has become very cheap in the past few years.

Build your Contingency Fund and get out of debt. Your Contingency Fund should be your first priority for all the reasons outlined in chapter 6. Unfortunately, you don't have time to devote your attention to just one area at a time. So at the same time you are saving for emergencies, you must pay off your unsecured debt (chap. 7). Once you are free of debt, you're ready to devote 10 percent of your annual income to some combination of a 401(k), Roth IRA, and personal investing.

Your thirties matter because these are the years that you'll make the big financial decisions of life—kids, house, and career. This is the busy decade, and with all of the joy and high-speed living that comes with raising a family, it's easy to lose sight of planning for the future. I know how easy it is to assume there will be plenty of time for that later.

If you're nearing the end of your thirties and have to admit you've not begun to prepare for retirement, don't despair. But understand that you need to get started right away. Your first step is to drastically reduce your expenses to free up money to catch up.

In Your Forties

By now you are well seasoned and used to contributing regularly to tax-advantaged retirement accounts, and if you have children, you're also saving for college. Here's the amazing thing. If you bought a home when you were thirty, and bought a house equal to half the amount you were approved for but paid the higher payment every month, you could well have that home paid for in your forties.

On the other hand, if you have not yet started to prepare for retirement, this is your make-it or break-it decade. This is a crucial decade for building wealth. Your income is higher than ever, as is your net worth.

If you've racked up other debts, please listen to the siren call I'm sending across these pages. You are sacrificing your future joy to pay for all kinds of things you may not even have anymore. This is serious. Do whatever you must to get those debts paid off as quickly as possible. It makes no sense at all to pay double-digit interest rates on unsecured debt.

If you started retirement planning early in your career, you should be in pretty good shape. If you've just started thinking about it, however, you have some major catching up to do. Decide that you will diligently save at least 10 percent of your gross income for retirement. If you don't do that now, you'll need to double that amount later. Yes, it will be a challenge, but you have no choice. You must do it, even if it means downsizing your home or working more. Your good health and maturity are definitely on your side.

Make retirement savings your main goal. This may sound counterintuitive when your kids are getting older and college for them is much closer than retirement for you. But beware of that trap. Make sure you are on track to secure your retirement before funding college accounts or (gasp!) taking out parental college loans. Do not gut your own future to ensure theirs.

Adjust college savings. Using current tuition costs plus projected inflation, check to make sure you are on track with college savings for your kiddos if that is something you plan to help fund. It might be time to have the talk about choosing a college you can afford, not the one they want to attend.

Invest. If your savings have grown beyond what you've needed to cover emergencies, you have a decent cash nest egg. It's time to aggressively build an index fund portfolio (chap. 10).

If you're feeling way behind due to what life has thrown at you over the past decades, it may be time for a serious look at your lifestyle to find all the places that money is leaking out of your life. By plugging those leaks, you will free up money to put into your emergency fund, pay off your debts, and fund your retirement savings. You still have years to work hard, but they are ticking off fast. Don't waste another day assuming things will just magically turn out okay. No one can promise you that.

In Your Fifties

This is the critical planning time. You still have ten to fifteen years to work, and you're reaching your peak earning. Your biggest expenses may be behind you (buying a home, raising the kids, paying for college), so you can reasonably devote more of your pretax income to retirement. Now's a good time to sit down with a fee-only planner (more on this in chap. 15). If you've been saving since your twenties, you'll enjoy seeing your diligence rewarded. If you got started late, it's time to step up your saving. Stay disciplined, even if that means making lifestyle sacrifices.

Play catch-up. If you are behind and if you qualify, consider taking advantage of the IRS catch-up contributions. Once you're fifty or over, you can contribute thousands more to your 401(k) plan than your younger colleagues. In 2012, you could have contributed an additional $5,500 over the annual limit of $17,000 for a total of $22,500.

Downsize. As your nest empties and those who return finally do leave, it might be time to downsize for convenience but also to cut expenses. The money you save by moving into a smaller home (taxes, utilities, maintenance) can be funneled into retirement savings.

Buy long-term care insurance. This is the time to consider this kind of insurance. You need to be in good health to qualify, but you don't want to take out a policy too early or you'll pay in for far too many years prior to making a claim.

Pay off your home mortgage. Make sure you are on track to pay off your home prior to the time you retire. If you are not on track, do everything you can to get on track.

Meet with a financial and estate planner. Now that you have amassed a sizable amount in your retirement account, savings account, and investment portfolio, you should consider meeting with a fee-only planner who can look at what you have and make strategic recommendations.

In Your Sixties

Traditionally, this decade will be all about retirement. But you may decide to work more years, either because you want to or because you need to. If you haven't even begun saving, you may need to delay retirement as long as your physical and mental health allow you to work. That's the price you pay for not having planned ahead. If, however, you have been steadily building a retirement portfolio, your accounts should be looking really good by now.

Zero in on living expenses. It's time to assess, or reassess, your retirement income needs to see if they are in alignment with the sources of income you'll have available in retirement. One rule of thumb is that once you retire you are going to need about 80 percent (plus more for inflation) of the amount you need to cover your lifestyle now. If you don't know how much you need to live now, you will have no good way to project your needs in retirement. Be sure to consider inflation while you continue to find ways to spend less. Never forget that it is a lot easier to cut expenses than to increase income or create a higher return on investments. A good saver will beat a good investor every time.

Weigh your Social Security options. You are eligible to file for early benefits at age sixty-two, but your monthly check will be reduced by about 30 percent for the rest of your life. Wait until your full retirement age (sixty-five, sixty-six, or sixty-seven, depending on your birth year) for full benefits, or until seventy to receive 32 percent more each month. But wait. There's a lot to consider before making that decision.

Figure out where you will live. You do not want to have a mortgage when you are no longer employed in retirement, so now is the time to reassess your housing situation. If you cannot see your way clear to repay it in full so that you own your home free and clear, perhaps you should sell the home and move to an area where your equity will be sufficient to buy a home outright.

In January 2012, the monthly Social Security benefit was $1,230 per person receiving benefits.[1] A couple who each earns that amount would have a retirement income of $29,520 annually. Could you live on that? Take a look at these places where the median household income is lower than the average Social Security benefit for a two-earner couple: Auburn, AL; Blacksburg, VA; Boone, NC; Cheney, WA; Mount Pleasant, MI; Murray, KY; State College, PA; Sunland Park, NM; Syracuse, NY; and West Lafayette, IN.[2]

Every year, numerous publications and organizations, such as the American Association of Retired Persons (AARP) and *US News & World Report*, publish a variety of lists covering the best or the cheapest places to retire for the current or coming year.

Apply for Medicare health care. Ninety days prior to turning sixty-five, the window opens for you to apply for Medicare health care benefits. You can do this online at Medicare.gov. The process is remarkably easy.

If there is one thing we all possess as women (if you ask the men!) is the freedom to change our minds. What you did yesterday is not what you must do tomorrow. The course you set in your twenties is not your destiny in your forties. Embrace that thought, then determine right now that you'll do whatever you must to get on track with your own personal retirement planning.

15

How to Choose a Financial Planner

Never trust an advisor so much that you follow that person blindly.

Allan Roth, certified financial planner

Investing is not as much about doing math as it is about having confidence in your ability to read and follow directions. You really can manage your savings and investments on your own—at least I think you can. It just takes discipline and determination. And time.

That being said, there may come a time when you will want to hire a competent, trustworthy, unbiased, and well-informed financial planner to advise you. You'll know because (1) your debts are all paid or at least well under control, (2) you have a respectable amount in savings and a growing retirement account, or (3) you inherit an IRA or some significant amount of money.

A financial planner is a professional who can help define your financial goals, make sure you have the lowest-cost insurance, guide you into appropriate investments for your situation and your age, advise you on matters such as when to begin taking Social Security benefits, and advise you of the tax-saving strategies available to you.

But beware. Not all financial planners are honorable. Keep your eyes wide open. They can be masters at persuading themselves that what's in their best interest also happens to be the right thing for you to do. The fact that you're paying someone to help you gives you no guarantee that you will get good results. And just because you and a financial person with professional status attend the same church or a woman you met at the spa says her son-in-law is the best financial planner in town does not mean this person is right for you.

Financial Planners Come in Three Flavors

The services that financial planners offer can vary widely. Some financial planners assess every aspect of your financial life—including savings, investments, insurance, taxes, and retirement and estate planning—and help you develop a detailed strategy or financial plan for meeting all your financial goals. Other professionals call themselves financial planners, but they may only be able to recommend that you invest in a narrow range of products.

When hiring a financial planner, you should know exactly what services you need, what services the planner can deliver, and any limitations on what he or she can recommend. In addition, you should understand what services you're paying for, how much those services cost, and how the planner gets paid.

When it comes to financial advice, here is a good rule to follow: Accept advice but do not grant authority. Financial decisions need to be yours. Your advisor should give you all of the information you need to make your own decisions.

Financial planners vary not so much by the kind of advice they give but by the way they get paid.

Commission-based. This type of planner does not charge her clients for her time. You won't get a bill for an office visit or the number of hours she spends creating your financial plan. However, she will sell you investment products such as stocks, bonds, and insurance policies, and she will receive commissions on those sales. When you think about it, the commission-based planner has a significant conflict. If a planner earns a big commission when you buy a specific investment but a much smaller commission or none at all if you buy another, that's a pretty good incentive for her to steer you toward the one that offers her the better reward.

Fee-based. This type of financial planner works on a fixed fee or charges hourly for the service. The fee is stated up front. Even though this type of planner will make recommendations on the investments and insurance you should have, you'll be on your own to make those purchases if you decide you want them. For example, a planner could recommend that based on your season of life and how many people are dependent on your income that you need a $1 million life insurance policy or that it's time to purchase long-term care insurance. If you agree, then you will need to shop around to find the best deal on those insurance policies. With a fee-based planner, you are paying for advice and a personalized plan.

Fee-based planners deliver another key advantage. As registered investment advisors (RIAs), they are required by law to meet the fiduciary standard, which makes them legally responsible for putting the best interests of their clients ahead of all else.

If the fee-based planner you select works by the hour, you want to know how many hours you are talking about. Is there a cap? Can he or she just run up a huge bill? On the other hand, the financial planner who charges a fixed fee for services rendered sets that fee according to a percentage of the assets in question. One percent would be typical.

Combo. Yes, the third type of planner is a combination of the first two. You pay a fee, either fixed or hourly, plus the planner earns commissions when you move forward with purchasing financial instruments based on the advice you've paid for.

Here's My Advice

The fixed-fee planner is the type of professional I recommend. At a charge of 1 percent of your assets, this will not be cheap. In this scenario, the planner has no incentive to sell you a particular investment, but if your portfolio grows, so does the planner's annual fee. Even this arrangement is not 100 percent perfect. There could still be a conflict or two, and this is the reason I want you to learn all you can and stay involved in the decision-making process.

A financial planner is not a savior. This person is an advisor and not a stand-in so you don't have to do your own research. Think of him or her as a member of a team you coach. Each player has a specific job to do, but ultimately, you are the one who calls the shots.

Financial planners can:

- help you define your financial goals
- help you build a diversified, low-cost investment portfolio and stick to it

- make sure you have the lowest-cost insurance coverage you need
- help you make the best decisions with your Social Security benefits
- work with your tax professional to reduce the amount of tax you will pay on your investments through strategic, perfectly legal methods
- help you pass assets to your heirs, if that is your desire

Planners can't:

- pick winning stocks
- build wealth without requiring risk
- let you in on secret deals that are too good to be true

Six Questions to Ask a Potential Financial Planner

1. How would you describe your ideal client?

Any good financial advisor will have an area of expertise. You want someone who has expertise working with someone like you. If this person works with young families and you're five years from retiring, maybe this isn't the person for you. You want to find a financial advisor whose ideal client is very much like you in terms of age, stage of life, and asset level.

2. How long have you been a financial advisor?

You want someone who has at least five years' experience working as a financial planner. She might have years of experience as a CPA or in the mortgage or banking industry, but that doesn't mean she has expertise as a financial advisor.

3. Will you explain a financial concept to me?

You need to discover if you can understand this person's explanations. If he speaks over your head or makes no sense, keep looking. You want to work with someone who can explain financial concepts to you in a way you can understand. Here are a few such concepts to choose from. What is the difference between passive and active investing? How do you determine how much money a client can safely withdraw each year without running out of money? What is a laddered CD or bond portfolio?

4. What assumptions do you use to make retirement planning projections?

Part of the planning process will show you how much money you will have each year from the time you begin to live on your retirement money through your life expectancy. Of course your planner has to guess, so you want to know what rate of return she will use to project how your assets will grow, the rate of inflation, and your personal spending habits.

You want a planner with conservative assumptions, not pie-in-the-sky ideas to make you feel good. Better to end up with too much money than not enough. Here are conservative assumptions given the economic times in which we now live: growing financial assets at 5 percent a year, using an inflation rate of 4 percent (meaning your personal expenses will go up by 4 percent a year), and increasing the value of real estate assets on paper by 2 percent a year. If this person responds using 12 percent rates of return and 2 percent inflation, she is going to make things look a lot better than they really are.

5. Do you use low-cost index funds for your clients' portfolios?

If a financial advisor responds no and goes on to claim that he can pick stocks and funds for you that will outperform a portfolio of low-cost index funds, be wary. In fact, that would be a big red flag for me. If most fund managers cannot beat index funds (recall chap. 10), why would you believe this advisor can without working full-time on just your portfolio? I wouldn't put much faith in a financial advisor's claim that he can beat the market, even if he has done so on occasion in the past.

6. How will I pay for your services, and how will you be compensated?

This is not an unreasonable question to ask. There are three possible choices here: (1) You will pay an hourly fee (ask what that fee is), (2) you will pay a fee based on a percentage of your assets, or (3) you will buy financial products such as stocks, bonds, insurance, and so on, and the planner will earn a commission based on the cost of those products.

This is so important that I am going to say it again. An advisor's or planner's primary loyalty will be to the hand that feeds her. That is simply human nature. If she is paid directly by fees from you (hourly or a set fee), that planner will have an incentive to provide advice and service that are in line with your goals. If she is paid by commissions, she is first and foremost bound to the products her broker dealer (the firm that employs her) prefers her to sell.

16

Popular Ways to Commit Financial Suicide

We either make ourselves miserable or we make ourselves happy. The amount of work is the same.

C. Castenada

I love the cable show *What Not to Wear*. I can't say I've achieved wardrobe perfection, but I have become more aware of what constitutes a fashion risk. I believe I am making fewer fashion faux pas simply because I am more focused on the rules that hosts Stacy London and Clinton Kelly have drilled into my head.

In a similar way, I want you to become fully aware of "What Not to Do" in your financial life. Face it, we live in a fast-paced, peer-pressured, consumer-driven world. There are forces in play that have been carefully crafted to manipulate us to act and behave in ways that can be horribly damaging in the long run. The way to counter that pressure is to learn ahead of time what not to do and then to follow those rules.

Living on Credit

Debt, particularly unsecured consumer debt such as credit card debt, personal loans, student loans, and any other kind of debt that is not secured by real estate or some other asset of value, is like cancer. It starts small and can even remain manageable for a while. But then it begins to grow. If not treated aggressively, it can take over and do horrible things to your life. This kind of runaway debt that comes with high interest rates and relatively small monthly payments will sabotage any plans you have to save for retirement.

Once you cross the threshold where you are unable to pay your credit card bill in full in a single month, opting for the minimum monthly payment, you will have reached a dangerous place in your life.

Living an Overstated Lifestyle

According to columnist Ellen Goodman, "Normal is getting dressed in clothes that you buy for work and driving through traffic in a car that you are still paying for—in order to get to the job you need to pay for the clothes and the car, and the house you leave vacant all day so you can afford to live in it."[1] Been there, done that. Think about how stupid that is.

You may not be depending on credit to get from one month to the next, but you may well be spending every last nickel you have to keep up that pretentious lifestyle you created for all to see and envy. Sadly, many people prefer the trappings and illusion of wealth over the freedom of actual

153

wealth. They want to look wealthy rather than be financially mature.

If your leased cars, mortgaged furniture, private school tuition bills, cable TV, shopping sprees, and $300 monthly mobile data plans keep you from regularly giving, saving, and preparing for retirement, you're living way beyond your means. And for what? To impress the neighbors? To make sure your family looks good at church and community events? The truth is that you are headed for financial disaster. When it hits, it won't be pretty.

An understated, frugal lifestyle, in which you give, save, and live below your means, is the best environment in which to raise kids and save for retirement. And it's the best environment for truly enjoying life and being of service to others too.

Stripping Home Equity

Lenders love to push the idea of accessing your home's equity as the solution for credit card debt. Parents often look to home equity as the perfect source to pay for a wedding or college tuition bill. Homeowners look to their equity as the best way to pay for an addition or a much-deserved swimming pool. I think all of those ideas are lousy because they can lead to a very bad outcome.

If you move debt to your home in this way and then cannot keep up with those big payments, you'll lose your home through foreclosure. Stop looking at your home's equity as a pool of money you can't wait to get your hands on. Buckle down; get serious about paying off your credit cards now. Stop looking for shortcuts and phony fixes. Start paying and stop charging, and I think you'll be excited to see how fast you can get out of debt.

Raiding Retirement Accounts

When it comes to your employer-sponsored retirement plan, you can't have your cake and eat it too. You cannot take advantage of the benefits of investing your untaxed income and also have unrestricted access to the funds. The money you are investing in that plan is for retirement. The government allows you to invest pretax dollars. But here's the deal: You must relinquish access to that money until you reach retirement age.

Most retirement plans allow you to borrow from your account for immediate needs—which is, in my opinion, unfortunate. Although taking a loan may seem like an easy way to cover a big expense, it has serious drawbacks.

Once you take money from the account, you stop growth momentum. If the stock market rises before you repay the funds, you will miss out on a portion of the gains you would have earned. That could be significant if you take the full time allowed to repay the withdrawal. Never forget that it is not the amount of money you put into the account that makes the difference. It's the compounding growth over a long time that is going to turn your meager deposits into something glorious by the time you retire.

If you raid your retirement account and then leave your employer for any reason before you repay it in full, most plans require you to pay off the balance within thirty days. If you can't come up with the money, the loan may be considered a taxable distribution. That means you'll owe income taxes on the unpaid balance, plus a 10 percent penalty if you are younger than fifty-nine and a half.

If you take a loan from your employer-sponsored retirement plan, you are obligated to repay those pretax dollars with after-tax dollars. But the government won't take that into account when you retire. You'll have to pay tax again on that money when you withdraw it later. Double taxation is a severe penalty!

When you borrow from your plan, you are in effect spending your retirement savings during your working years. But even worse, if repaying the loan becomes a heavy burden, you may be tempted to reduce or eliminate your regular monthly contribution altogether. Even the slightest disruption in your savings plan can put your future security at risk.

If you fail to save enough money during your working years, you've lost your chance. You cannot go back and make things right. Your options will be severely reduced, and you may have to keep working longer than you'd like.

Don't think of your retirement account as a liquid asset. It is a frozen asset that is out of reach for now. Direct your energy instead toward reducing your expenses. Living beneath your means will eliminate the temptation to borrow from your retirement account.

Taking Out College Loans

Parent Loans for Undergraduate Students (PLUS) are non-need-based loans made to the parents of undergraduate students and one of the most popular ways that parents fund their kids' educations. These loans are guaranteed by the federal government and are processed much like a consumer loan, meaning they carry high interest and are unsecured.

Qualifying for these dreadful loans is dependent on the borrowing parents' credit ratings, but you do not need a high score to land one of these loans. PLUS loans do not have a stated maximum amount. Parents may borrow up to the difference between education costs and their student's loans every year, and for multiple students. Repayment begins two months after the loan proceeds are disbursed and must be repaid within ten years.

I don't even know where to start with pointing out the problems with PLUS loans. Let's start with the fact that such loans often come at the same time you need to be saving for your retirement years. Then let's talk about you not being able to foretell the future. You might believe with all your heart that repaying that ginormous PLUS loan within ten years will be no problem. But you don't know if you will have a job next month, let alone five or ten years from now. Adding the weight of a PLUS loan to your financial obligations could easily put retirement savings on hold.

Let me give you a quick account of a family I heard from recently. The family breadwinner was well along in his career, making close to a quarter of a million dollars annually. Admittedly, they ratcheted up their lifestyle to match their impressive income, believing there would be no way but up in the future. But then the kids needed to attend college, and the parents had not been saving for this. Their solution: Have the boys take out student loans in their names with the parents taking on the balance needed for both in the form of PLUS loans. Dad promised that he and Mom would take responsibility to repay all of the loans so their sons would come out of school debt-free. It all sounded great and remarkably easy.

The boys did graduate, but while they were in school, Dad lost his job. Unemployed for many months, he finally landed a new position but at a much lower salary—a drop of more than 66 percent from the salary he had when he and Mom so graciously took on all that debt.

Of course, the parents defaulted on the PLUS loans during the time Dad was unemployed, and they defaulted as well on the promise to pay the sons' loans. But does any of that make the loans go away? Oh no. It only makes them grow bigger, faster.

All of the unpaid interest and fees are added to the outstanding principal in a kind of reverse compounding. The loans grow monthly as the past due amounts are added to the outstanding balance. By law, these debts cannot be erased in bankruptcy court. Only the death of the student, in the case of the student loans the sons took out, or the death of both parents for the PLUS loans will forgive the outstanding balances.

The parents are simply unable to keep up with the payment schedule on all of these loans. As I write, one of the young men has a part-time job as a food server; the other cannot find a job. Both have moved back home with Mom and Dad.

If you want to help fund your children's college educations and you can do so with cash while remaining faithful to your own retirement saving, that's one thing. Going into debt to do so is quite another and one of the worst things you can do when it comes to planning and saving for retirement.

There are no laws or societal norms that require parents to pay for their children's college educations. In fact, doing so may be bad for the kids because it prolongs dependence on their parents, delaying the day they reach full maturity. Credible research suggests that students who pay their own way through school appreciate their education more than those who get it handed to them.[2] Refusing to take on PLUS loans is one way you can make sure you do not become a burden to your adult children in the future. Instead of strapping yourselves for many years to come with big monthly PLUS payments, you will be in a position to divert that money into your own retirement savings. That's a gift your kids may not understand or appreciate now, but just wait. That day will come.

Procrastinating

Many women incorrectly assume that it will be easier to save money for retirement later in their careers rather than when they are young and poor, so they procrastinate. It may be easier, but that is irrelevant if your true goal is to find the easiest way to a secure retirement. A secure retirement requires you to begin saving now whether it is easy or not. Procrastination is just wealth suicide on the installment plan.

The old way of thinking was to pay off the mortgage, pay for the kids' college, and then save for retirement. That worked fine when life expectancies were much shorter. But nowadays you may spend almost as many years in retirement as you did in your career. As a result, you need a bigger nest egg than previous generations needed to fund those extra years. A bigger nest egg requires a more aggressive approach to retirement savings while you are still working.

If you don't start saving now, you are throwing away the power of compounding returns, which is one of the most powerful tools in your arsenal for achieving financial security. The sooner you begin saving, the less you must save each month to reach any given savings goal, making the process easier to accomplish. The longer you wait, the more you must save each month, making it harder to get started and harder to reach your goal.

You can rationalize not saving now because you believe you will have lots of time to do it later. But that excuse doesn't

159

matter. The mathematics of how wealth compounds doesn't care about excuses. It's just math. When you throw away time, you throw away money.

If you grow your retirement savings at 10 percent compounded and wait just seven years to begin, you will end up with half as much money compared with if you started today. That can make the difference between spending your retirement greeting shoppers at Walmart or playing golf at your local country club.

17

Preparing for the Unexpected

In their hearts humans plan their course, but the LORD establishes their steps.

Proverbs 16:9

Things happen in life that we simply cannot prevent. You can't cheat death, accidents happen, and not all jobs or marriages last. But arming yourself with financial knowledge, creating a private credit history, purchasing the necessary insurance, and saving can make the difference between spending your retirement years in financial hardship and enjoying the best that your later years have to offer. No one can predict the future, but you can plan for the unexpected and help to ensure that you are protected no matter what lies ahead.

We make our plans then walk by faith, never knowing for sure what a day may bring. I don't suggest we need to be fearful about every possible thing that could be waiting around the bend. But just as with all of the plans we make for the future, we need to be ever mindful that life can change dramatically in a moment of time.

The events that create financial disasters for women are generally not the things we want to think about—the death of a spouse, a divorce, a serious illness, a disabling accident, or the loss of a job. While it is easier to think these things will not happen to us, life-altering events can, and do, happen anywhere, anytime. These events are surprising and upsetting, but that doesn't mean they have to be financially crippling.

Good planning can help prevent a personal tragedy from becoming a financial disaster. You can prevent a financial disaster by making sure you have good, basic information to help you make informed choices as you prepare to protect your future.

Here are six steps you can take to become more financially independent.

1. *Maintain good records.* Be sure you have copies of all current assets, bank account numbers, safe deposit information, insurance beneficiary information, IRAs and other retirement account records, tax returns going back seven years, mutual funds statements, stocks and bonds, health insurance policies, home owner's and auto insurance policies, the lease or mortgage information for your home, wills, trusts, powers of attorney, and birth and marriage certificates. It is also a good idea to keep receipts of major appliances with information on warranties.

2. *Have your name on all bank accounts.* If your husband dies suddenly, it could be very difficult to keep everything current if the checking account is in his name only. If you are married, you should also open checking and savings accounts in your own name just in case a will is contested or some other complication arises.

3. *Manage your own credit.* Good credit is essential to any sort of financial independence. Get credit in your own name through a personal credit card. Without good credit, it will be nearly impossible for you to borrow money to purchase a home or car, or even get a credit card, without assistance. A growing number of companies check credit reports before making hiring decisions. Landlords want to see a clean credit report before deciding who gets the apartment. The practice is called "risk-based pricing," and it is perfectly legal.

Like it or not, banks, credit unions, credit card companies, and auto financing companies look to credit data to set interest rates. Most banks now require a credit check to open a checking account.

Good credit means more than just paying your bills on time. While that is a critical part of maintaining a good credit rating, you must also check your credit reports every year to make sure there are no inaccuracies.

Credit scores range from 300 to 850. You'll need at least a 720 FICO score (MyFico.com) to be considered for any type of mortgage, but in order to get the best rates and most favorable terms, you'll need a score over 760.

The first step in managing your credit is to find out what's in your three major credit reports. You have a legal right to review all of the information the three big credit bureaus have collected in your name. And you need to do this because credible evidence suggests that most credit files contain misinformation and mistakes. Your report may contain a lot of negative data that belongs to someone else and was simply misfiled. No one cares about that except you, which is why you must assume the role of manager of your own credit.

Start by ordering your three free reports at AnnualCredit Report.com. This is the official site that complies with the federal law and the only place you can start the process to get your free reports. Once at this site, follow the prompts. You will be sent to the sites of the credit bureaus, but as long as you entered from the AnnualCreditReport.com site, you will not have to pay. You may also receive your annual complimentary copies of your three credit reports by calling 877-322-8228 or by sending your request to Annual Credit Report Request Service, P.O. Box 105281, Atlanta, GA 30348-5281. You will have to reveal your name, current address, Social Security number (don't worry, they already have it), and other personal identifying information.

If you are able to identify yourself to the satisfaction of the three credit reporting agencies (Equifax, Experian, and Trans-Union) by correctly responding to security questions, you can get your free credit report online within a few minutes, downloaded to your computer. If not, you will be instructed to call a toll-free number to speak with a customer service agent. You will also find instructions for how to proceed if you prefer to receive your free credit reports by mail.

Once you have a credit report in hand, look at this as you would a rap sheet. These are allegations that others have made about you that may or may not be true. Your job is to make sure the information is accurate. You will receive instructions with each credit report for how to dispute any inaccurate information.

4. *Assess your insurance needs and buy enough to protect yourself.* There are four kinds of insurance every family should have: life insurance, home owner's (or renter's) insurance, health insurance, and auto insurance.

Term life insurance is relatively cheap and something you need to fit into your budget. You need a policy for six to eight times the breadwinner's annual salary. If you are not employed but your death would put your children and husband in a tough financial position because they would have to hire others for child care and housekeeping, you need a policy that would cover all of these additional expenses for at least five years.

5. *Create wills for both you and your spouse.* Make sure you have a notarized original copy, a lawyer has a copy, and there is a copy in a safe deposit box. Review and update your will every five years or when you acquire significant new assets. While state laws vary, surviving wives usually inherit at least half of their husband's estate. However, given the nature of the modern family, inheritance can be contested by stepchildren, children, siblings, and even cousins. While a jointly owned house will automatically go to the partner who survives, no one wants to inherit a house only to find she cannot afford the taxes that go with it. It is very important to state clearly whom you want to receive your property and possessions. If both parties die at the same time, a will is important to make sure the surviving children are cared for and that assets are fairly distributed among survivors.

6. *Save, save, save!* One reason for the high rate of poverty among older women is the lack of personal savings. Every spouse, with or without income, can open a Spousal Roth IRA. The only requirement is that your husband earns enough income to cover the contribution. As long as your husband earns $11,000 in income, he can put $5,500 into his Roth IRA and $5,500 into yours (or $6,500 if either of you is over age fifty and earns at least $13,000).

18

Faith and Finances

Trusting God completely means having faith that He knows what is best for your life. You expect Him to keep His promises, help you with problems, and do the impossible when necessary.

Rick Warren

I laughed when I saw a cartoon of two career-type women, both dripping in bling and overly coiffed, chatting over lunch in a chichi restaurant. One says to the other, "Well, I have a faith-based retirement plan. I have faith that somehow everything will just all work out." Ha-ha. That's a good one.

But then I started thinking. That sounds like my retirement plan. I'm making reasonable preparations for retirement, avoiding debt and living below my means while paying off our mortgage—then trusting God for the outcome.

As I am writing this, the United States is still in recovery mode following the most significant economic downturn since the Great Depression. Unemployment seems stuck on high, while the housing market inches its way back to prosperity. Whatever today's or tomorrow's economic problems may be, I know that God is much bigger than all of them. He's greater than any economic crisis and knows with certainty what lies ahead. He promises never to leave me or forsake me, to be the same yesterday, today, and forever. This is why I am making reasonable preparations for retirement while not obsessing about it and trusting God for the outcome.

It wasn't until I'd wasted many years and made some really dumb choices that I finally learned how God feels about money. The most surprising thing for me was that God knows about my needs and cares about my wants. Money is important to God, so it's right that it should be important to me too.

The Bible is chock-full of financial advice—advice on how to get out of debt, how to stay out of debt, how to become financially stable, how to save, how to spend, how to prosper, how to invest, how not to waste your money, how to make the most of it, and how to have your money work for you.

Many of the money principles are more than suggestions or guidelines. They're laws. God's laws. Just as in your day-to-day life, where you can choose to obey or disobey laws that govern society, you can choose to obey or disobey God's laws on money.

Jesus often taught through stories known as parables. One of these stories is known as the parable of the talents (see Matt. 25:14–30). In this teaching story, Jesus gave us four principles or money laws.

But first, a little background. A talent in biblical times didn't refer to your awesome ability to play Beethoven's Fifth on the harmonica, although that would be considered quite a talent. A talent was equal in value to 130 pounds of gold.

Today, at about $1,750 an ounce, we're talking about $28,000 for one pound of gold times 130 pounds. Roughly speaking, one talent today would be worth $3,640,000—more than three and a half million dollars!

Now that we have an idea of what Jesus was talking about in terms of money, let's look at the story.

Jesus's Money Lesson

A wealthy businessman decides to go on an extended trip. Rather than put his money into the bank for safekeeping, he calls in three of his employees. He tells them he's leaving for a while and gives them the job of taking care of his wealth. The guy hands over bags of gold to them (each bag weighing one talent), but not in equal amounts. He trusts them with his wealth according to their ability to manage money.

The servant who is given five bags of gold to manage goes out and puts his money to work. He doubles the five bags to ten bags (that's $36,400,000 if you're counting). The next servant gets two bags of gold, and he does the same thing. He invests the money and doubles it to four bags of gold, or $14,560,000.

The third servant is scared of the stock market and the real estate market—and isn't even sure about the loan market. Cowardly, he digs a hole and puts the one bag of gold into the ground where it will be safe from thieves.

After a long time the master comes back and calls the servants in for an accounting. The first and second servants report that they doubled the money. The man is pleased with their results, thanks them for their hard work, and promises that since he knows how much he can trust them he will put them in charge of even more of his wealth in the future.

Then he calls in nervous Ned. I can almost see Ned standing there all sheepish and ashamed. Ned owns up to his fears, telling the master he was so afraid of losing the gold that he hid it in the ground to keep it safe.

I'm sure this wimpy guy was hoping against hope that he'd at least get an "attaboy!" for returning the entire amount safely to its rightful owner. But no. Not a chance.

The master is more than a little bit disappointed. "You wicked, lazy servant! I taught you to sow, gather, and then harvest to increase your holdings. But did you do what you were taught? No. Worse, you weren't even responsible enough to put the gold in the bank, where it could have earned interest. That would have been better than nothing" (paraphrase of Matt. 25:26–27).

What comes next just floors me. Not only does the master take the money from Ned, but he gives it to employee number one—the guy who turned his five bags of gold into ten. I don't know why that is so shocking to me, because I have to admit that if I were the master, I'd do the same thing. After all, if the first servant is that smart with money, I'd want him managing my wealth too.

We find the hook of the story in verses 29–30: "For whoever has will be given more, and they will have an abundance. Whoever does not have, even what they have will be taken from them. And throw that worthless servant outside, into the darkness, where there will be weeping and gnashing of teeth."

Did you get that? He called Ned a worthless servant. See? Money is important to God. In fact, I would say God is quite passionate about it and becomes displeased over the mismanagement of it, as evidenced by the weeping, gnashing of teeth, and utter darkness.

Jesus didn't tell his disciples this story to amuse them. Let's take a look at four financial principles in this story.

God Is the Source

If you see your employer, your spouse, your investments, your trust account, your parents, or any other entity as the source of your income, now and in the future, you are setting yourself up for a great deal of worry. Employers go away, parents and spouses die, investments can turn sour overnight. The truth is that all of these are only conduits in the delivery system. They are the channels through which you receive money, but they are not the ultimate source.

God, who gave you the intelligence, ability, and skill to think and work is the source of your money. Money is the method by which God meets your needs for food, shelter, and clothing. And when he gives you more than you need, he has expectations for how you will care for those resources.

Grabbing onto this truth will bring a sense of peace and calm to your life. No longer will you fear a drop in the stock market or the plunging of real estate values. No longer will you lie awake worrying about losing your job. The way your money is delivered may change radically and frequently, but the source never changes. It is the same yesterday, today, and forever.

Everything I Have Belongs to God

Nothing you have belongs to you. God owns it, and then he loans it to you for the seventy or eighty years you have on earth. You arrived with nothing, and you're going to leave in that same condition. All of us are on a short layover here on earth, a blip on the screen of eternity.

That job you have, that paycheck—they aren't yours. Neither is the trust account your parents set up for your education. Or the car you drive or even the home you purchased. Your health, intelligence, skills, abilities, relationships, and opportunities don't belong to you either. God is watching closely to see how you're taking care of everything he has entrusted to you. The sooner you learn this truth so well that it engulfs your every thought, the sooner you will enjoy the freedom God has for you to be the best manager possible of all the blessings he has for you both now and in the future.

Money Is to Be Used

God expects us to use and invest what he's given us to manage. Money is a tool to be used wisely, not hoarded, buried, obsessed over, or stockpiled. As we think about retirement, this is such an important principle.

In the parable, the master gave three rewards to the two honorable servants: (1) They received praise and affirmation, (2) they got promotions with greater responsibility, and (3) they received an invitation to celebrate.

What you do with money reveals your true character. The way you use it says a lot about who you really are and what you value.

Money Is to Be Saved and Invested

Money is a tool to be invested, not buried. Saving and investing are honorable methods by which to prepare for your retirement needs in the future. This way your kids, church, or society won't have to provide for you. That's the loving and responsible way to operate as a wise money manager.

God sees your life on earth as one event, not a series of pay periods. He sees what challenges lie ahead; he knows the number of your days. He's been providing for your present and your future all along. He is watching to see how you manage the money that comes into your life. If you spend it all, saving nothing for emergencies and investing nothing for the future so that you just limp from one paycheck to the next, you need to ask yourself just how trustworthy you are.

Let me illustrate this. Let's say your child, who is a reasonably mature fourteen-year-old, requires $45 per month to pay for her school lunches. You could give her the $45 at the beginning of the month with instructions for how to manage it so that she has enough to pay for the very last meal of the month. That would take some teaching and a lot of trust, depending on the maturity and ability of the child.

You decide to give it a try. You pony up $45 on the first day of the month and give clear instructions you are convinced she understands fully. You're determined to keep a close eye on this situation to ascertain if you can trust her to follow your instructions when there are so many things that could distract her now that she has money in her possession.

She buys lunch the first day but then sees a really cute blouse on day two. She spends the balance of her money, and you learn a lot. This child needs more instruction and practice before she can be trusted with the entire amount.

You go over the rules again, this time dividing the month into weeks. You hand her $11.25 to buy lunch for one week. This time she makes it through Wednesday, but somehow the rest of the money manages to disappear. She did somewhat better, but still she demonstrated she cannot yet be trusted with that much money. You patiently continue but with full knowledge that if she keeps flunking your tests, your trust in her will diminish proportionately.

It would not be at all unreasonable for you as the parent to determine that for now this child can only be trusted to manage her lunch money one day at a time. If you trust her with more, she breaks your rules and spends it on something else. Your heart aches, because at her age you believe she should be mature enough to manage her lunch money and even more, like maybe her clothing money. Perhaps even more than that. You'd love for her to demonstrate that kind of maturity. In fact, you'd be thrilled to turn a lot more of your resources over to her care, if only she could see beyond her selfish wants and desires.

Let me ask you: How much can God trust you? Have you demonstrated that you can be faithful with much? Or are you on some kind of week-by-week, hand-to-mouth, paycheck-to-paycheck kind of program?

You might say that if God were to hand you a boatload of money, you'd turn into an awesome manager on the spot. With your measly weekly paycheck, you haven't been given a chance to do that. Right? Well, let's see just how much he's entrusted to you so far. Take your annual household income and multiply that by your age minus twenty-one. Let's use $50,000 as your income and forty-seven as your age.

$50,000 x [47–21] = $1,300,000.

That looks like quite a large sum of money to me. It's a very rough estimate of the amount of money that has come into your possession and for which you have made decisions on where it should go. I can hear your objections. "I haven't always had a household income of $50,000 (or insert your dollar figure of choice)!" You're right, but this is an estimate to illustrate a principle. If your figure is different, it's still a large number. And I deducted the first twenty-one years of your life. I suspect if you could come up with an exact figure for our little exercise here, it would be significant.

While we're doing math, let's look at another number. Let's multiply your current household income by fifty years, a realistic working career in the United States.

$$\$50,000 \times 50 = \$2,500,000$$

This number does not take into account any promotions, raises, or increases. It's simply a ballpark figure, and a low one at that, given the span of half a century. There is no doubt that you are managing a fortune, which you're receiving incrementally over a long period of time. And I say this even if you do not have a job in which you earn your own income. You may be a stay-at-home mom or simply do not work for one reason or another. You're still part of a household, and, as such, I assume you have a say in how your family's resources are allocated.

Although the numbers may be fictional, they illustrate a stunning truth: You've been entrusted with a lot of money, and you will be entrusted with more in the future. Look, I'm the last one to point a finger. It is the sorrow of my life that I wasted so much time and so much money. I was a miserable failure as a steward whom God could trust. But I found forgiveness and redemption.

Reminds Me of a Joke

As the story goes, Rachel was a very devout woman. One day, she found herself caught in a flood. When the water was up to her knees, a neighbor came by in a rowboat and offered her a ride to safety. Rachel replied, "No, thanks. I believe God will take care of me."

The water continued to rise, and Rachel found herself crawling up a ladder to the roof. When she reached the roof, a sheriff in a boat came by and offered to take her to safety. But Rachel told him, "No, thanks. I believe God will take care of me."

Soon the sun began to set, darkness was all around, and Rachel found herself sitting on the highest point of her roof, her feet in the water. A rescue helicopter came by and lowered a ladder down to Rachel. But Rachel shouted, "No, thanks. I believe in God, and he will take care of me."

The waters kept rising, and eventually Rachel drowned. When she got to heaven, Rachel went to God and said, "I don't understand. I tried to be a devout woman. I was faithful, believed strongly, and prayed constantly. And yet I am dead."

In a loving but irritated tone, God replied, "What more would you have me do? I sent two boats and a helicopter!"

Okay, it's a joke, but it speaks so much truth. God promises to meet our needs and tells us not to worry about the future. He knows the future. He sees what we will need not just today but even into retirement. He has been providing for our futures all along—in this week's paycheck and next year's bonus. And every day for years and years he has done that for us.

But even though God provides, we must also do our part. We must be good and faithful stewards. Saving for the future is not contrary to trusting God to provide. Saving and planning are marks of a responsible and trustworthy steward and a response to God's faithful provision. God longs to bless us more and more as we become more trustworthy and financially mature.

I have lived in the darkness of greed and debt. And I've lived on the receiving end of God's promise to reward trustworthiness. I highly recommend the latter.

Just Enough Light

Years ago, my husband and I were driving through California's Mojave Desert at night. It was my turn to drive, while he slept. Let me tell you, it was dark!

What struck me in the black stillness of the night was how the headlights were not lighting the entire way. Those two beams of light illuminated about thirty feet in front of us. From my spot behind the wheel, I could easily see where the light ended. But as I moved into that light, the light moved ahead just a little bit more—lighting the way to our destination thirty feet at a time.

Playing a game of chicken with myself, I got up the nerve to turn off the headlights for a couple of seconds just to see how dark it really was. Not a good idea. Intellectually, I knew we would be fine for just a few seconds, but my brain could not overcome my emotions. Instant panic sent chills down my spine.

Without the light, we would have come to a complete stop—stuck in the middle of the desert until daybreak. Those two beams from the headlights gave me all the light I needed to move forward the next thirty feet and the next until we reached our destination.

I know I will never find peace by obsessively attempting to control or predict what will happen to me in the future. When my mind spins out of control with multiple scenarios,

I feel peace slipping out of my grasp. The truth is that I cannot figure out the future. And when I try, I only drive myself crazy with anxiety and worry.

God does not reveal what is ahead, but he faithfully gives just the amount of light we need to take the next step and then the next. What a perfect antidote for anxiety and fear.

I believe I honor God when I make saving, investing, and planning for retirement a part of my stewardship. I cannot see the destination from where I am now, but I continue making plans with confidence and wisdom. Then I hand my plans over to God, trusting him for the outcome.

19

What You Need That
Money Can't Buy

Glance at the past. Work in the present. Focus on the future.

Todd Stocker

There is no doubt that accumulating an appropriate amount of money for your retirement years is inescapably important. But growing a big nest egg should not be your only retirement goal. With such a narrow outlook, you could find yourself with an impressive stream of income but living a very miserable existence. There really is more to retirement than just money.

These factors are equally important for a happy and satisfying life at any age but especially in retirement:

- good health
- relationships
- meaningful activities

A satisfying retirement will be shaped more by what you do today than by what you hope your life will be like years from now. You don't need to look into a crystal ball to see what your life will be like. Just look in the mirror. That's the best way to predict what your life will be like then. Don't like what you see? Start making changes now.

Every day you are becoming the person you will be. That can be depressing or very exciting. It's up to you. You can't afford to wait until you turn seventy to begin making your retirement a time of joy and fulfillment. You can start living to your maximum potential right now, developing many areas in your life so that you will move seamlessly from your current lifestyle into the way you will define retirement.

Care for Your Health

Dr. Thomas Perls, lead author of *Living to 100: Lessons in Living to Your Maximum Potential at Any Age*, says that many people still believe the myth that the older you get the sicker you get, when in fact his studies and those of other researchers reveal that it is much likelier that the older you get, the healthier you've been.[1] By investing in your health now, you can greatly improve your odds of enjoying retirement once you get there.

According to Miriam Nelson, professor at the Friedman School of Nutrition Science, research shows that your current lifestyle is far more important than what you did when you were younger. This is not to say that if you are in your twenties or thirties you don't have to be concerned a bit about healthy living. The point is that as we age, the body's capacity to get stronger and to be healthier and happier is still there.[2] Even in middle age, it's not too late to reverse the damage created by an unhealthy lifestyle.

Still, old habits can be tough to break. Don't assume you can wait until you're sixty-five to start exercising and eating right, then quickly reverse the results of decades of bad choices. That is not going to happen. So start today. If you're unwilling to make healthy choices now, you can bet it's not going to get any easier in years to come.

Nurture Your Relationships

If you plan to enjoy retirement, start building strong relationships now. Studies have shown that the most powerful predictor of life satisfaction after retirement is the size of your social network. In fact, those who were more satisfied with life had networks of about sixteen people on average, while those less satisfied with life had fewer than ten.

It's not the size of your financial portfolio but the number of friends and family with whom you hold a strong bond—whether that network includes your family, your church, or your cycling club—that predicts how happy you will be after you retire.[3] Your close family and friends will be an essential and comforting aspect of retirement.

I will concede that it's not easy to maintain an active social network during your younger years. Making a living and dealing with day-to-day events can easily absorb all your time. Yet ignoring social contacts at the expense of growing your nest egg can backfire when you find that it's difficult to renew relationships that have become stagnant or been allowed to die. If you don't have time to nurture relationships with friends and family now, don't assume they will have time for you later. The solution is to find a reasonable balance between growing wealth and maintaining a network of friendships. You simply cannot afford to sacrifice one for the other.

Engage in Meaningful Activities

Every now and then, do you catch yourself dreaming of being free to follow your passions without worrying about getting up in the morning to go to a job? I sure do.

Retirement may give us that freedom. Staying physically and mentally active by engaging in activities, hobbies, and pastimes that we find enjoyable will have other benefits as well. This kind of mental stimulation can reduce the risk of age-related health problems such as heart disease, type 2 diabetes, and Alzheimer's disease.[4] But we simply cannot afford to wait until we retire to get active. Develop lifelong interests and activities now.

You may not have what it takes to pursue something like golf or cycling by the time you turn in your employee badge. Now is the time to become the person you plan to be, remember? It's time to break out the clubs and find that bike helmet. Or take up knitting or kite flying. Or figure out how to knit and ride at the same time! That's what I'm trying to figure out.

You may not have as much time for pleasure now as you will then, but now is the time to figure out what you love to do that will keep you active both in mind and body. I think it's fair to assume that none of us wants to become the typical American retiree who watches 29.4 hours of TV each week[5] and takes advantage of few, if any, learning opportunities.

Here are six ideas for staying active now and right on through the day you retire.

Pursue a hobby. Everybody needs a little something they love to do that just makes them happy because it's enjoyable. For me it's knitting. And baking bread, quilting, and roasting coffee. And I love to putter in the garden when time allows.

I have so many hobbies that I may be forced to retire just to get all that enjoyment in.

You don't have to be crafty to find a hobby. You can join a book club or travel group. The point is to dig deep to discover that thing you do that makes you want to get out of bed in the morning.

Pick up a sport. Physical activity and fun do mix well. But you need to have a proclivity toward being somewhat athletic. If you feel competitive, pick up a sport such as golf, bowling, or racquetball. If you aren't into sports per se, you can keep your muscles and bones strong by weight training at the gym or joining an exercise class. Health clubs are good places to hang out with physically fit people who can motivate you to stay in shape. Take a dip in the pool or sign up for a yoga or tai chi class. Or go all out and train to run a marathon. Start now and you can jog right into retirement.

Volunteer. Imagine how you might be able to bless others with your wisdom, experience, and strong mind when free time becomes more plentiful. Choose a cause you're passionate about and volunteer your services. Consider short-term mission trips to expand your horizons and stimulate your mind. Volunteering will challenge your mind and keep you involved in the community, all while helping others. And you don't have to wait until the day you retire. In fact, volunteering well before you retire gives you time to look for a group that can make good use of your existing skills. It also lets you find out whether you're really suited for a particular type of work and gives you a chance to look elsewhere if you aren't. You may discover that you need additional education or training to do volunteer work that will be truly satisfying.

Another reason to start volunteering before you retire is that finding a cause you can truly bond with is sometimes harder than you might think. But don't get discouraged. Find ways now that you can be useful to another person or organization. Giving back is going to give you a whole new outlook and appreciation for all the ways you have been blessed.

Hang out with active people. Hanging out with active people will make you get active or be left behind. Make friends with people who are active and plan outings with them. Choosing to be around active people encourages you to stay fit to keep up.

Play the piano. This is the ticket if you want to keep your brain active. Learning to play the piano has been documented to promote physical rehabilitation in people of all ages, but it can especially help older adults stay mentally active and protect against certain illnesses such as Alzheimer's disease.[6] Start fresh with a teacher who specializes in beginning adults or dredge up your old piano books and dust off that keyboard. Whatever your level of proficiency, get playing!

Educate yourself. If you can't handle the music, pick up a second language or pursue some other field of learning. Studies show that speaking more than one language can delay the onset of Alzheimer's disease. Basically, the brain grows and thrives when it is confronted with new information—new words, new tasks, new sensory experiences. Unused and unchallenged, the part of your brain that carries messages back and forth will begin to shrink and disappear.[7] Learning a second language also stimulates the development of new nerve connections in your brain and keeps your memory sharp.[8] You'll probably be welcome everywhere from your local college to community center.

As cliché as it may sound, retirement is not a destination; it's a journey. By beginning your journey today, you'll be a seasoned, well-rounded, and happy traveler when you cross the threshold to retirement.

20

Smart Women Are Doers

You don't become what you want, you become what you
believe.

Maya Angelou

Where I live in Southern California, earthquakes are
prevalent. Seismologists tell us that we experience
hundreds of quakes nearly every day. They're small, and we
don't feel them. But still, the earth moves regularly.

I live sixty miles to the west of one of earth's major faults,
the San Andreas Fault. Scientists say that we are way overdue
for the Big One, and they're talking about an earthquake of
at least seven points on the Richter scale. They're not talking
theoretically. Statistically, they say, it is coming. A devastating
major earthquake will hit where I live.

Do I believe it? Well, sure I do. Everyone I know does too.
The Big One is coming. But you should wonder if I really

184

mean that. Why? Because I don't do anything that proves my belief to protect myself, my family, or my home. Okay, I have a small stockpile of food and a windup radio, but that's about it.

If I truly believed the Big One is coming soon and will devastate everything in its path—destroying my home and possessions and killing me and my family—I would have moved to stabler ground far away in another state a long time ago. Now, this doesn't mean I don't kinda sorta believe. I'm agnostic about it. I'm not really sure.

I believe the science that says it could happen, but I don't believe it is going to happen to me with 100 percent certainty. That makes it so easy for me to push it out of my mind to allow room for things more urgent, like a new roof. That's a "real" need, while relocating to escape an earthquake isn't so much.

Sadly, this is the way a lot of women think of retirement. Sure, it's probably going to happen some day, but not anytime soon. They may assume that their husbands have this retirement thing all covered; maybe they'll win the lottery or get a big inheritance. Who knows? Somehow it will all work out. It's so far away and other things are so much nearer that they become slightly agnostic, which means they're not sure what they believe.

It doesn't matter what we say we believe. The truth is that we only truly believe the things we do. What I've learned is that most women are not doing anything to plan for retirement, for any number of reasons. Perhaps they don't really believe there is a need or that they will ever face that season of their lives. Smart women, on the other hand, are strong and willing to face the future, no matter how challenging.

Smart women are doers. We know and believe that retirement in some form lies ahead for us, and we are ready to take responsibility for getting ready for it, no matter our current age or stage of life. Aren't you relieved to know that we are not part of the 92 percent of women who do not feel they're smart enough to reach their retirement goals? Not only are we ready, but we are willing and able too. We're smart women!

In the months between my shocking wake-up call (chap. 1) and this moment as I write, I have done more retirement planning than you can imagine. I'm talking about catching up—in spades. My life has been impacted in ways I could never have anticipated, and I am so grateful. I pray that the same is happening for you and that you've already begun to think hard about your own retirement planning.

If you truly believe the day will come when you will not have an income on which to depend, your best course of action is to start doing something about it now. If you believe that the earlier you begin the easier it will be, you will prove it by doing it.

So are you ready to start doing? I don't know the details of your life, how you manage your finances, or what steps, if any, you have taken so far to get ready for retirement, but here are three things you can do this week to get started.

1. *Have the talk*. Set a time this week to have a conversation with your husband (or if you are single, a close friend or relative) about planning for retirement.

2. *Make a list*. Think of all the things you would like to learn and do once you have more free time than you have now. Pick one or two that you can start doing now in preparation for a seamless transition to retirement.

3. *Create a plan*. Review the six strategies (chap. 3) and make a simple plan for how and when you will implement them. Start with your money management system. If you are

happy with the system you use now, move on to the second strategy. If not, make finding a free checking account the first item in your plan.

If you are interested in continuing a dialogue about your journey and plans for the future, I would love to hear from you: mary@debtproofliving.com.

A Short History of Retirement

Retirement is a rest stop for people starting something new.

Unknown

Retirement has become the status symbol of a life well led. It's the culmination of the American dream. The message is that if you can just hang on long enough, an idyllic life awaits in which you travel a lot, play golf whenever you want, and finally get to do all the things you've been putting off because your job kept getting in the way.

You probably know of people who are retired and are thoroughly enjoying their lives of leisure. I do too. They do all of the things they love with what appears to be a great deal of ease. And we know of others who are not doing so well in retirement. They retired too early or with too much debt. They've taken on too many family members' financial difficulties or found their resources cut in half due to death or divorce, but the bills and debts remain in full.

While retirement may have various meanings and understandings depending on whom you talk to, for our purposes, retirement is that life event when you leave your job and retreat to your home, where you live off your 401(k) account or pension and your Social Security benefits. That might be when you reach full retirement age or not. A person who is independently wealthy may choose to retire at age thirty-five, then live her life in service to others.

The age at which you will retire is not as much of a given as it once was. And it is not as certain as it once was. Some people will never retire, and not because they die young, but because they will be financially unable to survive without continued employment.

So the question is not, Will retirement happen for me? Yes, retirement will happen for you. One way or another, should you live a long life, the day will come when you are no longer willing or able to work for a living. The real question is, How is it going to look? In the answer are many questions, which I hope this book answered for you.

It's likely that you have friends, family, and acquaintances whom you've watched retire with monthly pension checks, full health care benefits, IRAs, investment portfolios, plus Social Security. They're enjoying life without a care in the world—at least that's the way it looks from the outside. Things are changing rapidly, and we need to look to both the past and the future to be as prepared as possible.

A History of Retirement in the United States

Not so long ago, retirement was not the American dream it is today. In fact, the idea of retiring from work is a relatively new invention. Retirement was never designed to help older people; it began as an effort to get them out of the workforce.[1]

For much of history, life meant birth, a brief childhood, work, and death. People were farmers, shopkeepers, or artisans—or the wife of one, in which case you raised the kids and carried out all things domestic. If you lived, you worked. There was no such thing as retirement. You stopped working when you were dead or could not be repaired.

Even in biblical times, it was customary to carry on until you dropped regardless of your age, unless you were a temple priest, in which case you were to retire at age fifty and work no longer.[2]

The industrial revolution brought with it demands for efficiency, and older workers didn't fit the model. Retirement laws were enacted so older workers had no choice but to quit their jobs in exchange for a small company pension—so small that it was not unusual for retirees to move in with their working sons or daughters, adding their small pensions to the family household. That was the general way of life in America until the Great Depression, which changed everything.

The 1930s were a period of widespread political, social, and economic upheaval. Unemployment reached 24.9 percent in 1933. Older people were seen as a burden and were often fired to get them out of the way so the younger set would have opportunities to work. And that created a new problem. If you forced people to retire at an early age, there needed to be a way to make sure they were taken care of.

The Social Security Act of 1935 provided the necessary guarantees. Another result was to reduce unemployment by permanently removing the large numbers of older people from the workforce.

With passage of the Social Security Act, older Americans were expected to stop being productive in exchange for their monthly benefit checks. The understanding was that they would spend that money, which would increase consumption in the economy from which they had been dismissed. Incidentally, when Social Security began, life expectancy for a man living in the United States was 59.9 years, and for a woman it was 63.9 years.

During the Great Depression, millions of workers of all ages lost their jobs. But World War II turned it all around. Suddenly, young, old, men, women—anyone who could work—did work. The war put America at full employment again.

When the war ended in 1945, millions of young men returned from Europe and Asia. They all needed jobs, of course. The women and older people who had worked on the home front during the war were expected to step aside for the returning veterans. Mandatory retirement laws gave companies the legal right to give older workers the boot to hire returning veterans. Older workers were up in arms over this idea of having to leave their jobs. They believed that work was central to life, and many refused to apply for Social Security.

Overwhelming resistance to mandatory retirement was strong. But mandatory retirement rules gave corporate America, labor, and the federal government something that each of them wanted. They needed to find some way to change the attitude of older workers. What they needed was a new definition of retirement.

The term *senior citizen* was introduced as part of a huge marketing campaign funded by the insurance industry to replace the less appealing designation of "old-age" pensioner. Designed to convey a mature, responsible, and disciplined person who knew his or her place in society, a new message extolling the joys of leisure bombarded older workers. Retirement is your well-earned reward for years of dedicated service! You're entitled to it!

Organizations and magazines encouraged this blissful image. It worked. By the late 1960s, the idea of retirement as well-deserved leisure had been completely assimilated into the American consciousness. Retirement became a full-fledged industry. And older people accepted the idea that work after age sixty-five was no longer desirable or even realistic. Slowly but surely retirement became part of the American dream— every citizen's just reward and not just a clever way to get rid of unwanted workers.

Now that nearly everyone was retiring at sixty-five, the consequences began to pile up. Retirees needed money to live on. Having a pension became a necessity. But fewer than half of working Americans were participating in an employer-sponsored pension plan.

To make matters worse, weak pension rules, guidelines, and rights of employees in the 1970s meant that many people who expected to be eligible for pensions found they had next to nothing once they retired. As a result, most people relied on Social Security as their primary source of retirement income. But Social Security provided only a bare minimum. A huge number of retired Americans found themselves teetering on the brink of poverty.

In 1978, a provision was added to the Internal Revenue Code to allow taxpayers a break on deferred income, or money earned but not yet received. It didn't get much attention until 1980, when Ted Benna figured out how this provision could be used to create an easy, tax-advantaged method to save money for retirement. It wasn't until 1983 that the government moved quickly to authorize new types of pensions, which are now generally known as 401(k) plans, after the paragraph in the tax code that gives them tax-deferred status.[3]

The switch from defined benefit plans (in which the employer funds the plan) to defined contribution plans (in which employees kick in their own funds) happened quickly. By 2006, over 75 percent of workers had defined contribution plans.

Workers were encouraged to invest their 401(k) assets in company stock or other equities. Things were good when the stock market was heading up but soured quickly when the market tanked.

Over the next forty years, people over sixty-five will come to account for over 20 percent of the US population. The over eighty-five age group will be our fastest-growing age segment. By 2050, people over eighty-five will be as large a percentage of the population (4.6 percent) as people over sixty-five were in 1930.

At the heart of America's economic problems are two programs, Social Security and Medicare. Most Americans are counting on Social Security for at least a portion of their retirement income and on Medicare for their retirement health care. I have little worry that current recipients will see any reduction in benefits. For those not yet retired, my best guess is that the program will be there in some shape or form, but how that will look is anyone's guess.

So what?

You may not care one bit about the history of retirement in the United States. But you should if for no other reason than to realize just how much the government can control retirement issues by enacting, amending, and repealing laws. The government, in effect, holds the purse strings on trillions of dollars in individual retirement accounts. Changes to the laws could have a huge effect on 401(k) and IRA accounts.[4]

Mark Twain is often credited as saying, "History does not repeat, but it does rhyme," which I find to be strikingly apt. With unemployment rates stuck on high and the US economy having such a hard time recovering from the Great Recession, it's not difficult to see eerie similarities to the 1930s.

Retirement Options

Retirement is not a constitutional right; it's not a civil right or a human right. It is not even a God-given right. It's a modern option, a lifestyle for people who have accumulated enough money to pay their bills every month without an ongoing paycheck. Retirement as we know it comes in multiple flavors.

Voluntary retirement. You come to the point in your life when you have amassed sufficient assets and financial resources to support yourself and pay all of your bills for the rest of your life without the need of a paycheck. So you quit your job and go on what is in effect a permanent vacation. It is a choice you make.

Medical retirement. Due to failing health, it becomes too physically and/or mentally difficult to continue in your job, or in any job for that matter. Even if you do not choose to retire, retirement chooses you.

Phased retirement. Becoming more popular these days, phased retirement is when, depending on your needs and preferences, you move into a new part-time career, a seasonal job, or a relaxed work schedule, typically with your current employer. You choose to phase into voluntary retirement.

You might work on a project basis, which allows you to take off several months each year. Or you may try a one-year sabbatical. The possibilities of phased retirement are wide open. A phased retirement doesn't necessarily mean you continue to work for someone else. You can start your own business, work part-time in a different field, switch to a different company, or even try making your hobby your business. Phased retirement is a way to ease into retirement in a way that makes sense financially as well as mentally and physically. Working longer means you get to add more to your nest egg while also delaying withdrawing from it.

Delayed retirement. With fewer companies offering pensions, 401(k) plans returning sometimes disappointing results due to volatile investment markets, and Social Security's uncertain future, many Americans now face the prospect of working well into what used to be thought of as "the golden years." About one-third of Americans say they will need to work "until at least eighty" to live comfortably in their retirement.[5]

Forget retirement. This is where I fit. I'm very fortunate. I do work that I love, that requires no physical labor, and that has no mandatory retirement age. The planning I'm doing is for when I become incapacitated and make a move into assisted living. Otherwise, I plan to keep writing until I drop.

Notes

Preface

1. Linda J. Waite and Maggie Gallagher, *The Case for Marriage* (New York: Broadway, 2000), 67.

Introduction

1. www.dol.gov/ebsa/publications/women.html.
2. www.globelifeinsurance.com/article/Could-You-Live-On-Social-Security.
3. KC Diwas, "Learning from My Success and from Others' Failure: Evidence from Minimally Invasive Cardiac Surgery," Harvard Business School, July 19, 2012, www.hbs.edu/research/pdf/12-065.pdf.

Chapter 2: You've Already Got What It Takes

1. US Department of Commerce Economics and Statistics Administration, "Women in America: Indicators of Social and Economic Well-Being," 2011, www.whitehouse.gov/sites/default/files/rss_viewer/Women_in_America.pdf.
2. "Women: Let's Talk about Retirement," the 12th Annual Transamerica Retirement Survey, www.transamericacenter.org/resources/TCRS12thAnnualSurveyWomenReport.pdf.
3. Willard F. Harley Jr., *His Needs, Her Needs* (Grand Rapids: Revell, 1986), 125.
4. www.barclayswealth.com/Images/BWA-Barclays-Wealth-Insights.pdf.
5. Doug Hirschhorn, "Think like a Woman and Make More Money," *Forbes*, November 5, 2011, www.forbes.com/sites/doughirschhorn/2011/11/05/think-like-a-woman-and-make-more-money.
6. www.womenshealthmag.com/life/money-and-women?cat=26235&tip=26239.

Chapter 3: A Lifetime Money Plan

1. Reuters Health Information, *Social Science and Medicine* 50 (2000): 517–29.

Chapter 4: Develop a Money Management System

1. www.schwab.com/public/schwab/banking_lending/checking_account.
2. www.usaa.com/inet/pages/bank_checking_main?wa_ref=pub_global
_products_bank_checking.
3. www.ally.com/bank/interest-checking-account/?INTCMPID=HP_NAV_CHK.
4. www.smartypig.com.
5. www.capitalone360.com.
6. www.mvelopes.com.
7. www.mint.com.

Chapter 5: Put Your Money Management System to Work

1. Elizabeth Warren and Amelia Warren Tyagi, *All Your Worth* (New York:
Free Press, 2005).

Chapter 8: Maximize Your Retirement Accounts

1. United States Department of Labor, www.dol.gov/ebsa/publications/10_
ways_to_prepare.html.
2. www.irs.gov/Retirement-Plans/Amount-of-Roth-IRA-Contributions-That
-You-Can-Make-For-2013.
3. Ibid.
4. www.cnn.com/2012/06/27/opinion/hiltonsmith-retirement-savings/index
.html; www.demos.org/publication/retirement-savings-drain-hidden-excessive
-costs-401ks; and www.gao.gov/assets/600/590359.pdf.
5. AARP, www.aarp.org/work/retirement-planning/info-02-2011/401k-fees
-awareness-11.html.

Chapter 9: Own Your Home Outright

1. "Coldwell Banker Survey Reveals 2012 Housing Trends," www.coldwellbanker
.com/real_estate/learn/coldwell_banker_survey_reveals_2012_housing_trends.

Chapter 10: Build Your Personal Investment Portfolio

1. www.forbes.com/sites/rickferri/2012/10/11/indexes-beat-active-funds
-again-in-sp-study.
2. www.cbsnews.com/8301-500395_162-57561584/another-poor-showing
-for-active-managers.
3. http://us.spindices.com/documents/spival/persistence-scorecard-december
-2012.pdf?force_download=true.
4. http://personal.vanguard.com/us/whatweoffer/mutualfundinvesting/
indexandactive?Link=facet.
5. http://search.fidelity.com/search/getFundFactsResults?question=spartan&
refpr=rmf1&refpr=MFRes_001&MFff=spartan.
6. www.schwab.com/public/schwab/investing/accounts_products/investment/
mutal_funds/index_funds.

Chapter 11: How Much Will I Need to Retire?

1. Here's one for your consideration if you are interested in a scientific stab at your life span: http://gosset.wharton.upenn.edu/mortality/perl/CalcForm.html.

2. www.fidelity.com/inside-fidelity/employer-services/age-based-savings-guidelines.

3. www.statefarm.com/learning/life_stages/retire/estimate_needs.asp.

4. http://money.cnn.com/2012/07/12/pf/expert/preretirement-income.moneymag/index.htm.

5. www.ricedelman.com/galleries/default-file/ipf09_08.pdf.

6. Don't sweat the calculation. Use the inflation calculator here: http://buyupside.com/calculators/inflationjan08.htm.

Chapter 12: Can I Count on Social Security for My Retirement?

1. www.ssa.gov/oact/tr.

2. www.forbes.com/sites/janetnovack/2012/04/23/will-social-security-be-there-for-your-retirement.

3. www.nwlc.org/resource/women-and-social-security.

Chapter 13: The Value of Time

1. www.globalrph.com/davesfv.htm. This is the future value calculator that will figure out this calculation.

Chapter 14: Quick Guide to Planning by Decades

1. http://ssa-custhelp.ssa.gov/app/answers/detail/a_id/13/~average-monthly-social-security-benefit-for-a-retired-worker.

2. http://money.usnews.com/money/retirement/slideshows/10-places-to-retire-on-social-security-alone.

Chapter 16: Popular Ways to Commit Financial Suicide

1. http://en.wikiquote.org/wiki/Ellen_Goodman.

2. www.usnews.com/education/blogs/college-cash-101/2009/10/09/7-reasons-to-work-your-way-through-college.

Chapter 19: What You Need That Money Can't Buy

1. Thomas T. Perls, MD, MPH, et al., *Living to 100; Lessons in Living to Your Maximum Potential at Any Age* (New York: Basic Books, 1999).

2. Liz Szabo, "Will the Sins of Your Past Catch Up with You?" *USA Today*, December 27, 2005, http://health.groups.yahoo.com/group/hopeforhepc/message/2426?var=1.

3. Diane Swanbrow, "To Retire Well, Invest in Making Friends," *University Record*, September 16, 1998, www.ur.umich.edu/9899/Sep16_98/friend.htm.

4. "The Benefits of Physical Activity," Harvard School of Public Health, www.hsph.harvard.edu/nutritionsource/staying-active-full-story.

5. http://money.usnews.com/money/retirement/articles/2012/07/02what-retirees-do-all-day.

6. www.get-piano-lessons.com/learning-to-play-the-piano.htm.

7. http://e-healthtoday.com/artman/publish/article_14.shtml.

8. www.fi.edu/learn/brain/exercise.html.

Appendix

1. www.thenexthill.com/a-brief-history-of-retirement-in-america-part-1.htm.

2. "But at the age of fifty, they must retire from their regular service and work no longer" (Num. 8:25).

3. http://en.wikipedia.org/wiki/401(k).

4. www.gpo.gov/fdsys/pkg/CHRG-110hhrg44713/pdf.

5. www.wellsfargo.com/press/2012/20121023_MiddleClassRetirementSurvey.

Glossary

10-10-80. A money management system in which you divvy up your net income so that you give away 10 percent, save 10 percent, and live on 80 percent.

50 percent solution. A money management system in which your basic necessities or "monthly must-haves" consume 50 percent or less of your income. The other 50 percent is for fun and savings (emergency fund, retirement, short-term goals, etc.).

60 percent solution. A money management system in which you use 60 percent of your income for expenses, you save 10 percent for retirement, you invest 10 percent, you hold 10 percent for emergencies, and you spend 10 percent to enjoy life.

401(k). A tax-deferred savings and investment plan in which employees may choose to contribute up to about $17,500 (in 2013). The catch-up limit for anyone over fifty is $5,500, which means anyone over fifty can contribute $23,000 in 2013. Employers often match a percentage of an employee's contribution. Employees control how the assets are allocated among different types of investments. All taxes plus a 10 percent penalty are usually imposed on withdrawals made before age fifty-nine and a half.

American dream. The ideal that life should be better and richer and fuller for everyone, with opportunity for each according to ability or achievement regardless of social class or circumstances of birth.

annuity. A contract that guarantees fixed or variable payments over time. Some investors buy annuities to provide them with a stream of income in the future.

automatic debits. When you authorize service providers such as utility companies, insurance companies, and others you select to reach into your bank account and take the amount you owe automatically.

bond. A kind of promissory note that shows you loaned money to a company or municipality, which will be repaid with interest.

bounce protection. This is similar to overdraft protection, but the money to cover the overdraft comes as a short-term loan from the bank's money, not the customer's funds. Bounce protection is extremely expensive as it carries a high rate of interest plus a daily surcharge until the account is brought current.

catch-up. An IRS rule that allows people who are fifty or older to save more in their tax-advantaged accounts to make up for lost time during their younger years.

certificate of deposit (CD). A bank instrument that enables a depositor to earn interest on his or her money during a fixed period of time. The rate varies depending on the amount invested and the duration of the CD.

certitude. A word that is a cross between certainty and attitude; confidence, sureness.

compounding interest. As interest or growth occurs, instead of withdrawing that gain from the account, you leave it in to increase your principal. Now your interest begins to earn interest, and growth takes place exponentially.

Contingency Fund. A pool of money to be held for emergencies that is kept liquid, safe, and earning interest, if possible.

credit score. A three-digit number that measures a person's creditworthiness based on past behavior with money management. The higher the score the more creditworthy.

defined benefit plans. Pension plans that guarantee a specific retirement benefit.

defined contribution plans. Pension plans that require specific rates of contribution but do not guarantee a specific retirement benefit.

direct bank. A bank that does not have a building you can walk into. A direct bank, also called an online bank, is accessed via the internet.

direct deposit. When you authorize an employer or other to pay you by depositing funds directly into your bank account rather than with a paper check that you must then deposit into your account.

estate planning. Planning for the orderly handling, disposition, and administration of assets that are left behind after an individual's death. Includes drawing up a will, setting up trusts, and figuring out ways to minimize estate taxes.

Estimated Benefits Statement. A concise, easy-to-read, personal record of the earnings on which you have paid Social Security taxes and a summary of the estimated benefits you will receive when you're eligible to draw benefits.

expense ratio. This is the annual management fee charged to each shareholder of a mutual fund, expressed as a percentage.

FICA. The Federal Insurance Contributions Act is a US federal law that levies taxes to be paid out of every person's wages to support Social Security.

financial planner. A professional who can help define your financial goals, make sure you have the lowest-cost insurance, guide you into appropriate investments for your situation and age, advise you on matters such as when to begin taking Social Security benefits, and advise you of the tax-saving strategies available to you.

full retirement age (FRA). Also referred to as "normal retirement age" or NRA, this is the retirement age at which full retirement benefits will be received. FRA is sixty-five for those born in 1937 or earlier, sixty-six for those born between 1943 and 1954, and sixty-seven for those born in 1960 or later.

Great Depression. The economic crisis beginning with the US stock market crash in 1929 and continuing through the 1930s.

Great Recession. A term that describes the recession that started in December 2007. Generally, the Great Recession lasted longer and was more severe than prior recessions but did not eclipse the levels reached by the Great Depression.

high-yield savings account. A saving account that pays a higher rate of interest than is typical in a bank or credit union. This of course is relative, because what may have been considered high-yield ten years ago may be quite different from the best rate of interest available today. Still, a high-yield account pays more interest than is typical.

index fund. A type of mutual fund with a portfolio constructed to match or track the components of a market index, such as the Standard & Poor's 500 Index (S&P 500). An index mutual fund provides broad market exposure, low operating expenses, and low portfolio turnover.

inflation. The rate at which the general level of prices for goods and services is rising and, subsequently, purchasing power is falling.

inflation indexed. Benefits that rise over time to offset increases in the cost of living, usually as measured by the Labor Department's consumer price index.

investing. Putting your money to work in a commercial undertaking subject to some level of risk with the expectation of a reasonable return over time. The greater the return being offered, the greater the risk you are taking.

investment portfolio. A term referring to the entirety of your investments.

IRA. An Individual Retirement Account (IRA) is for any individual who has a taxable compensation or self-employment income who will not reach age seventy and a half by the end of the year. In 2013, IRAs let you save up to $5,500 a year, $6,500 if you are over fifty. All money contributed to an IRA along with whatever it may earn goes untaxed as long as the money is in the IRA. You can open an IRA at a bank or other financial services company that has received IRS approval to offer IRAs.

management software. Computer software that helps you track your spending, manage your bank account, and make a spending plan.

Medicare. A US federal government program of hospitalization insurance and voluntary medical insurance for persons who are age sixty-five and over and for certain disabled persons under sixty-five.

Mint. Online money management site that allows you to link all of your accounts in one place and then keep track of all your activities. With your Mint account, you can track your spending, keep an eye on your goals, and do better with your money.

mutual fund. An investment vehicle that is made up of a pool of funds collected from many investors for the purpose of investing in securities such as stocks, bonds, money market instruments, and similar assets. Mutual funds are operated by money managers who invest the fund's capital and attempt to produce capital gains and income for the fund's investors.

Mvelopes. Envelope budgeting software available at Mvelopes .com.

net asset value (NAV). This is the current amount that an investment is worth in real dollars. Your NAV will change on a daily basis, sometimes hourly.

net worth. This is the amount of money you would have left over today after you sold all of your assets and paid off all of your liabilities (debts). It is possible to have a negative net worth.

nonsufficient funds. A term that applies when a person writes a check or makes a debit purchase for more than the amount of money in the account; there are not sufficient funds in the account to cover the purchase or the draft presented for payment.

online bank. See **direct bank.**

online bill pay. The act of sending money to creditors and service providers by electronic transaction. Basically, you transfer the money out of your account into the account of the person you are paying. You skip all the paper—the payment stub, envelope, and postage stamp.

overdraft protection. A service bank's offer to their customers to cover their overdrafts from the customer's savings account or personal line of credit.

overdrafter. A person who habitually writes checks or swipes a debit card for more money than the account's current balance.

Parent Loans for Undergraduate Students (PLUS). Non-need-based loans made to the parents of undergraduate students and one of the most popular ways that parents fund their kids' educations.

pension fund. A fund set up and invested by an employer or a labor union to provide retirement income for workers. The funds accumulate income and capital gains tax-free, which are used to pay benefits.

power of attorney. Authorization of one person to make legal decisions and take other actions—such as signing legal documents—on behalf of another person.

Rapid Debt-Repayment Plan (RDRP). A simple and effective method by which to repay unsecured debt quickly.

refinancing. Revising a payment schedule, usually to reduce monthly payments. A common way to do this is to reduce the interest rate on a mortgage.

reverse mortgage. A home equity loan for people who are at least sixty-two that may allow a qualifying senior to stay in her home rent-free while using some of the money that purchased that home in the first place. A reverse mortgage does not have to be repaid until the borrower dies or leaves the property.

Roth IRA. A tax-advantaged account, this works differently than an IRA or 401(k) in that you deposit after-tax dollars. However, once the money is in the account, it and the gain over the years will not be taxed again.

secured debt. A debt that is secured by collateral such as real estate or an automobile. If the borrower fails to pay, the lender can sell the collateral to satisfy the debt.

simple IRA. Savings Investment Match Plan for Employees for companies with up to one hundred employees. Allows workers to put aside up to $6,000 per year; their employers can choose to match contributions dollar for dollar up to 3 percent of the worker's pay or make an across-the-board contribution of 2 percent to each eligible worker. Employers opting for the 3 percent match can cut it to 1 percent for two out of any five years.

Social Security. A US federal program of social insurance and benefits developed in 1935. The Social Security program's benefits include retirement income, disability income, Medicare, Medicaid, and death and survivorship benefits. Social Security is one of the largest government programs in the world, paying out hundreds of billions of dollars per year.

spending plan. A written plan in which you "pre-spend" your money before you really spend it, to give yourself a road map for where it will go. Some might call this a budget.

Spousal IRA. Every spouse, with or without income, can open a Spousal IRA. The only requirement is that the working partner earns enough income to cover the contribution. As long as your husband earns $11,000 in income, he can put $5,500 into his IRA and $5,500 into yours each year. If you are fifty or older, the amount is $6,500 each to allow for catch-up. You will deduct the contributions from your tax return, following all of the rules and guidelines set up by the IRS.

stock. A type of security that proves ownership in a corporation and represents a claim on part of the corporation's assets and earnings.

tax-advantaged account. This is a method by which the IRS allows a person to save and invest money that has not yet been taxed, such as 401(k) and IRA accounts. There are many rules and restrictions, one of which is that taxes are paid as the money is drawn out of these accounts, ideally after the account holder has reached age fifty-nine and a half. Prior to that age, there is a severe penalty to gain access to the funds.

tax deferred. An investment that accumulates earnings that are not subject to taxes until the investor takes possession of the earnings, often at a point at which the investor is in a lower tax bracket than before, such as retirement.

thrift saving plan. A savings and investment plan for federal workers.

unsecured debt. A debt you incurred with your signature alone, not by pledging collateral. Credit card debt and student loan debt are both examples of unsecured debt because there is nothing to be repossessed if you fail to pay.

vesting. Reaching the point, through length of service, at which an employee acquires the right to receive employer-contributed benefits such as pensions.

Index

Mary Hunt, award-winning and bestselling author, syndicated columnist, and sought-after motivational speaker, has created a global platform that is making strides to help men and women battle the epidemic impact of consumer debt. Mary is the founder of Debt-Proof Living, a highly regarded organization consisting of an interactive website, a monthly newsletter, a daily syndicated column, and hundreds of thousands of loyal followers. Since 1992, DPL has been dedicated to its mission to provide hope, help, and realistic solutions for individuals who are committed to financially responsible and debt-free living.

As a speaker, Mary travels extensively, addressing conferences, corporations, colleges, universities, and churches at home and abroad. A frequent guest on radio and television, she has appeared on dozens of television shows, including *Dr. Phil*, *Good Morning America*, *The Oprah Winfrey Show*, and *Dateline*.

Mary lives with her husband in Orange County, California.

Want more debt-proof tips and tricks?

Explore DebtProofLiving.com/SmartWoman to find bonus material including:

- Slow cooker recipes
- New tools to help manage your finances
- Homemade laundry detergent recipe that fights stains and overspending
- Information about joining the new Retirement Forum
- And more!

Debt-Proof LIVING

Debt-Proof LIVING

Debt-Proof Living is a great big wonderful community offering help and hope to anyone who wants to learn how to manage their money more effectively. If you want to get out of debt—or stay out—and learn how to live below your means, Debt-Proof Living is the place to be.

Debt-proof living is a way of life where you spend less than you earn; you give and save consistently; your financial decisions are purposeful; and you work toward your goals by following a specific plan.

DebtProofLiving.com is the home of the debt-proof living philosophy. It is primarily a member-only website with features ranging from money management tools, articles, resources, community forums, consumer tips, recipes, and more. Here you'll find, in continuous publication since 1992, the DPL newsletter, which is published in an online format available to all members of this website.

Visit DebtProofLiving.com today to find out how you can debt-proof your life!

"Simple rules of the road that cut through confusion, mystery, and misery."

—Lisa Rose, founder, First Friday Women

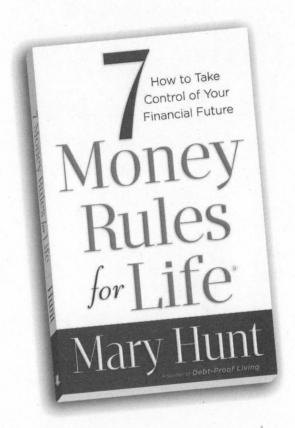

Mary Hunt, nationally syndicated financial columnist and founder of Debt-Proof Living, distills over 20 years of experience into seven simple principles that help people get out of debt and manage their money.

Christmas—with no debt, less stress, and more joy!

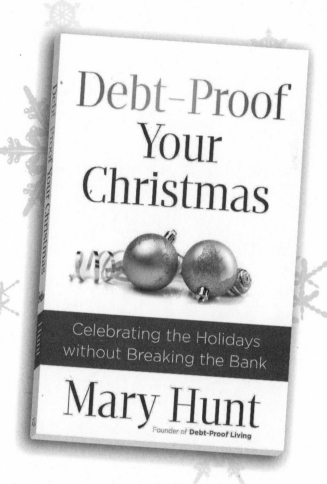

Mary Hunt shows you how to assess your situation, commit to no new debt, and think creatively about gifts.

"Simple, time-tested financial plan for kids."

—Dr. Kevin Leman, *New York Times* bestselling author of *Have a New Kid by Friday*

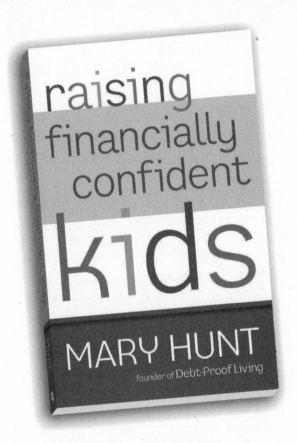

Drawing from solid statistics and her own hard-won knowledge and experience, Hunt helps parents protect their children from the financial pitfalls of easy credit, an attitude of entitlement, and our culture's chummy relationship with debt.